The Guide for Entrepreneurs

HOW TO EXPORT

Everything You Need To Know
To Get Started

Roger
Fritz

PROBUS PUBLISHING COMPANY
Chicago, Illinois
Cambridge, England

© 1992 by Roger Fritz

ALL RIGHTS RESERVED. No part of this publication may be reproduced, stored in a retrieval systems, or transmitted, in any form or by any means, electronic, mechanical, photocopying, recording, or otherwise, without the prior written permission of the publisher and the copyright holder.

This publication is designed to provide accurate and authoritative information in regard to the subject matter covered. It is sold with the understanding that the publisher is not engaged in rendering legal, accounting, or other professional service.

Authorization to photocopy items for internal or personal use, or the internal or personal use of specific clients, is granted by PROBUS PUBLISHING COMPANY, provided that the U.S. $7.00 per page fee is paid directly to Copyright Clearance Center, 27 Congress Street, Salem, MA 01970, USA. For those organizations that have been granted a photocopy license by CCC, a separate system of payment has been arranged. The fee code for users of the Transactional Reporting Service is 1-55738-215-8/92/$00.00 + $7.00.

ISBN 1-55738-215-8

Printed in the United States of America

IPC

1 2 3 4 5 6 7 8 9 0

Dedication

For Nancy & Susan

Who will see a world of nations brought closer together each year because of one thing—the benefits of trade.

CONTENTS

Preface   vii

Chapter 1
    What in the World Is going On?   1

Chapter 2
    Is Export for You?   17

Chapter 3
    Setting Up Your Business for Export   41

Chapter 4
    Get Set . . . Go!   55

Chapter 5
    Managing the Business   75

Chapter 6 After the Sale	105
Chapter 7 Other Avenues to Pursue	117
Chapter 8 Help From Your Home State	125
Chapter 9 Uncle Sam Will Help, Too	145
Appendix A State Contacts for Export	165
Appendix B Export Glossary	219
Index	233
About the Author	239

Preface

The central message of *How to Export* is that U.S. business can no longer afford to ignore opportunities in other countries.

In proclaiming that message it has a single purpose—to help companies sell their product or services in other countries. The first priority is to point the way for those who have not begun this exciting venture. The second, of almost equal importance, is to stimulate and enhance the success of those who have started but only scratched the surface.

Export opportunities for American businesses have never been greater. The need is urgent if we are to counter the tremendous gains already made by some other countries.

How to Export was *not* written as a theoretical treatise on the economic, strategic, political, or foreign policy implications of increasing exports. Rather, it contains practical, specific, pinpointed advice and references which will enable business owners, managers, and product and marketing specialists to determine what to do about exporting—when and where.

We will:

- stress how small businesses can get started and why selling overseas need not be the exclusive domain of huge companies;

- point to *specific* local, state, national and international contracts;

- detail how to determine profit potential;

- pinpoint specific requirements for financing, documentation, shipping and customs; and

- provide the information needed for licensing and joint ventures.

Above all, I wanted to take the mystery out of exporting, and to stimulate as many readers as possible to get going in foreign markets. Here, in one place, are the steps to be taken, along with advice on how and where to take them.

We have a long way to go, and others are outpacing us. In whatever ways *How to Export* accelerates the process of catching up and moving ahead, I will feel a special reward.

The work of Don Young has been indispensable in this project. His knack for organizing vast amounts of material in a usable format is a reflection of skills honed over decades of firing-line experience. They are prized and appreciated.

Roger Fritz
Chicago, Illinois

CHAPTER 1

WHAT IN THE WORLD IS GOING ON?

Most probably the world has never seen a peacetime period in which so many crucial events are occurring in so many places at virtually the same time as there are today.

Some might even argue that the word "peacetime" is superfluous and that there is more being done today to reshape the world than at *any* time in the past, during peace or war.

On virtually every continent and in nearly every nation, major political, social, and economic changes are taking place. They are occurring even as you read these words—some of them with heart-stopping suddenness, their ramifications breathtaking, their scope absolutely mind-boggling.

There can be no doubt that these events will impact, in one way or another, *every individual in the civilized world.* How they impact you will be no less significant than the way in which they will impact your business, whether you are a small entrepreneur or the executive of a large corporation.

Those who respond to these changes quickly and in an appropriate manner will realize the greatest benefits. Those who do not will find a place waiting for them next to the buggy whip and gas-light manufacturers of the past.

1992

Even as World War II was winding down, far-sighted observers realized that, one day, the nations of Europe would rebuild, realign and (quite probably) unite. That was the historical precedent and the predictable future. Thus, the European Economic Community (EC) was formed in 1957.

The modern EC has four parts: an executive branch (the Commission), two legislative branches (the Council of Ministers and the Parliament), and a judicial branch (the Court of Justice). It includes 12 member-nations: Belgium, Denmark, France, Greece, Ireland, Italy, Luxembourg, The Netherlands, Portugal, Spain, The United Kingdom, and West Germany; and, since the Lome convention, 60 African, Caribbean and Pacific nations.

In 1960 the European Free Trade Association (EFTA) was organized. It includes six members: Austria, Finland, Iceland, Norway, Sweden, and Switzerland. The organization started gradually reducing customs duties and quantitative restrictions on industrial products between member-nations, and by 1966, all such tariffs and quotas had been eliminated. In 1973, EFTA entered into free trade agreements with the EC, and since July 1976 all trade barriers between EFTA nations and EC nations have been removed.

Still another group, the Organization for Economic Cooperation and Development (OECD), was established in 1961. Headquartered in Paris, it is comprised of 25 member countries.

Notwithstanding all of this frenetic activity, economic world leadership now reflects the increasing influence of a new contender—Japan. Political leadership, once the dominion of Spain, France, and England, until recently was shared largely by the U.S. and the Soviet Union. The power once wielded by Roosevelt, Churchill, DeGaulle, Stalin and Hitler now rests in the hands of Bush, Major, Mitterand, and Kohl.

In 1985 the Commission of the European Economic Community recommended to its Council of Ministers that steps be taken to create a unified market throughout Western Europe by December 31, 1992! This recommendation led to the Single Europe Act, which took effect in July 1987. Since that time, the nations of Western Europe have set upon an ambitious program to:

> Set standards, testing procedures, and certification for products in 35 categories from toys and measuring instruments to cosmetics and quick frozen foods.

> Harmonize laws regulating company behavior including accounting operations, taxation, health and medicare, packing and labeling, consumer protection, insurance, and transportation across borders.

The Soviet Union responded quickly to the drive for economic unity in Western Europe. As early as 1988, they began to forge links between their COMECON organization and the West's EC. Within a year, trade agreements with both Hungary and Czechoslovakia had been negotiated with the EC.

In the United States, an interagency study group was formed to monitor and evaluate what is going on in the EC. Under the supervision of U.S. Trade Representative Carla A. Hills, specialists have been designated to answer questions in several key areas:

Agriculture
Rick Helm
U.S. Department of Agriculture
(202)382-1322

EC Treaty Obligations
Ted Borek
U.S. Department of State
(202)647-5242

Health and Environmental Regulations
William Bartley
U.S. Food & Drug Administration
(202)443-5470

Investment Issues
Margaret Fowler
U.S. Department of the Treasury
(202)343-9150

Quantitative Restrictions
Andrew Stoler
U.S. Trade Representative
(202)395-3320

Rules of Origin
Wendy Silberman
U.S. Trade Representative
(202)395-3063

Services
Fred Elliott
U.S. Department of Commerce
(202)377-4734

Societal Dimensions
Betsy White
U.S. Department of Labor
(202)523-6096

Standards Development, Testing, & Certification
Charles Ludolph
U.S. Department of Commerce
(202)377-5276

Third-Country Relations
Donald McConville
U.S. Department of State
(202)647-2320

In addition, the U.S. Department of Commerce has created the Single Internal Market: 1992 Information Service in the Office of

European Community Affairs, Room 3036, 14th Street and Constitution Avenue, NW, Washington, D.C. 20230, (202)377-5267.

The U.S. Chamber of Commerce, International Division, 1615 H Street, NW, Washington, D.C. 20062, (202)463-5460, has a business guide and a 30-minute video dealing with EC92.

The American Chamber of Commerce, Avenue des Arts 50, Boite 5, Brussels B-1040, Belgium, phone 011-32-2-513-68-92, publishes:

- Countdown 1992—a quarterly that reports on the status of all EC legislation. Price: $50 per issue.
- Business Guide to EC Initiatives—a publication which cites the content, prospects and implications to U.S. businesses of 76 proposed EC regulations. Updated twice a year. Price: $25.
- EC Information Handbook—an overview of the EC government and how it works. Describes several European groups involved in the process of shaping EC92. Price: $38.

Quite clearly, the impact of EC92 is enormous. A region that encompasses 320 million consumers, compared to America's 240 million and Japan's 120 million, Western Europe will be the world's largest free-trade market and could easily regain world dominance by the turn of the century.

Already, West Germany is the world's largest exporter. Combined, the member-nations of EC and EFTA generate a quarter of the world's trade.

The EC *today* exports 60 percent more than the U.S. and *twice* as much as Japan; while it imports as much as the U.S. and *three times* as much as Japan! It is America's top trading partner, and produced $161 billion worth of trade for us in 1988. Its annual production of $4.5 trillion worth of goods and services places it just behind the U.S. and way *ahead* of Japan.

Although there may be a great deal of potential behind the EC92 movement, will it ever actually materialize into anything? After all, the region is historically notorious for its fierce nationalism and for the protectionism it affords its industries, and there already are political and social grumblings over there, as well as business and economic ones.

Consider just a few of their achievements to date:

- In 1991 each country will recognize the university degrees of the others, enabling professionals to work anywhere in the EC. *Few American states offer that kind of reciprocity!*
- Major risk ensurers can now compete across national borders. *Don't try to drive in Mexico on your American Auto insurance!*
- They have established the ecu (European Currency Unit) as a common currency, and work is well along on forming a central bank.
- The framework is in place for forming a single European nation-state. Indeed, a proposal already has been made to allow Europeans to vote and hold municipal office not only in their home countries but *wherever they may live* throughout the EC.

What do the Europeans expect to gain from this effort? Primarily, of course, they are seeking to create a situation in which, if they do not actually *lead* the world economy, they will at least not be overcome by it. Individually, each member-nation has been beset by foreign competition, just as we have, and collectively they have decided that there is something they can do about it.

They are looking to hold on to their industries and their jobs. Indeed, certain projections indicate that EC92 will give them the means to boost their annual output of goods and services by 5 percent, increase employment by 2.5 million jobs, and reduce consumer prices by 6 percent.

Remarkable?—yes. Worth striving for?—definitely.

In many respects, the results are already beginning to accrue:

- In 1988, the EC's gross national product rose 3.7 percent to reach a 13-year high.
- Companies from outside the EC are *rushing* in to set up shops of their own or to buy an interest in existing EC companies. Why? In order to protect whatever share of the European market they now have and/or to establish a foot-

hold in the EC before "the floodgate opens" in January 1993.

The Collapse Of The Eastern Bloc

Throughout most of the 1980s, Western Europe made the bulk of the business news. Eastern Europe was going nowhere, and it seemed that everyone but the Soviets knew it.

During the 1980s, the U.S. created 36 million new jobs. Japan created nine million; West Germany, one million. In Eastern Europe, where unemployment often is against the law, everyone might have had a job, but few were actually working. There were shortages of everything, even if you went to the ever-present black market. The laws were repressive. Government officials were uniformly corrupt. Alcoholism was nearly epidemic.

In Eastern Europe, the postal and telephone systems were primitive, there were few radio and television stations, and the chief mode of transportation was the bicycle.

It was the Poles who revolted first. After years of defiance against the Soviets and against their own Communist government, the Poles ejected their old government, voted in a new one, and promptly announced their intention to compete on the free market.

In January 1989, the Polish government enacted a law that provides a three-year tax holiday for all joint ventures involving foreign participation.

These were bold moves for Poland. Productivity in its plants and factories is low. The country is $40 billion in debt. Inflation is running 600 percent per year. Over an eight-year period, Poland's average annual rate of growth has been only seven-tenths of one percent—except for Romania's, the worst in Eastern Europe.

Received with equal warmth was the news that many foreign investors were willing to participate in Poland's recovery. By March 1990, 22 American companies had offices in Poland, and a number of others, including Eastman Kodak, were exploring business options.

Italy's Fiat formed a joint venture with Poland's state-owned FSM auto plant and said that it planned to begin exporting over

50,000 Mickros automobiles to the West in 1991. The Mickros is the first all-new Fiat ever built outside Italy.

Japan's Daihatsu was considering a joint venture with an auto factory operated by Poland's FSO. Its production goal: 120,000 cars a year.

Next Came Hungary

In September 1989, Hungary opened its border with Austria and people began to pour into the West by the hundreds of thousands. Estimates given two months later indicated that East Germans alone flooded through Hungary and Czechoslovakia into West Germany at a rate of 200,000 a month.

Under a new Hungarian law, foreign investors can own 100 percent of a business enterprise—but only 72 percent if the firm is a privatized state enterprise. Joint ventures in electronics, pharmaceutical, packaging technology, biotechnology, tourism, and the production of vehicle components, farm machinery and food machinery are exempt from all taxes for five years and receive a 60 percent reduction in taxes thereafter. By 1990, $1 billion worth of foreign capital had been invested in 850 joint ventures. That same year, Eastern Europe's first stock market opened in Budapest.

Together Hungary and Poland will receive $840 million in U.S. loans before 1994. The Hungarian government has called for the withdrawal of all Russian troops by 1991. And, after 45 years, Hungary is poised to reestablish diplomatic relations with the Vatican.

All of this activity has not resulted in a miraculous turnaround for Hungary thus far. There have been too many years of Communist inefficiency and mismanagement. Production levels continue to be low. The average Hungarian factory worker earns just $140 a month. The country is $20 billion in debt—$2,000 per person. Hungary's largest creditor, with a due-bill for $6 million, is Japan.

Then Came East Germany

Russia's loss of control over Eastern Europe was symbolized most dramatically by the November 1989 breach of the Berlin Wall. It was as if the wall and the economic fortunes of the ten-nation Eastern Block collapsed simultaneously.

Even the Soviet Union, which had cut itself off from outside global commerce in 1949, was now declaring COMECON outdated and in need of a complete overhaul. COMECON had been based upon barter and artificial currency exchange rates; now the Russians proposed that all trade by 1991 should be conducted at world market prices and in hard currency.

Of all the countries in the Eastern Bloc, East Germany was in the best position to make the transition. Germany was different, after all—a twin that had been stripped from its sibling nearly 50 years ago. Many German families had aunts and uncles, brothers and sisters, cousins and in-laws on both sides of the now-corroded Iron Curtain. Here was a chance to become whole again.

East Germany also has the best industrial base in the Eastern Bloc, although its infrastructure is crumbling. German technology has always been strong. So too has the German work ethic. The East German standard of living is the highest in the Eastern Bloc, and the country's average annual rate of growth is also the highest—more than twice that of humble Poland.

Furthermore, West Germany is one of the richest and most productive countries on the continent. Its factories are operating at near-capacity, so new plants and a new source of manpower are most welcome—not to mention a new crop of consumers. Like the other East European countries, East Germany has suffered from a severe shortage of consumer goods.

Conceivably, West Germany could invest some $10 billion a year in its eastern neighbor, but the picture isn't totally rosy. Most of East Germany's state-run businesses have operated at a loss, and those losses have been covered by subsidies which, in 1988, resulted in a budget deficit of $70 billion.

It is no surprise, then, that East Germany, like all of the other Eastern Bloc nations, is in debt. The surprise is that the debt is a relatively low $20 billion.

Czechoslovakia, Bulgaria, and Romania Were Next

With all of the commotion going on elsewhere in the Eastern Bloc, the Czechs grew restless too. When 200,000 citizens demonstrated for the right to have free elections, millions of factory workers went on strike to show their support. And when the people got the opportunity to elect a new government, the leader of their choice was the one-time dissident Vaclav Havel.

Sixty percent of Czechoslovakia's gross national product comes from heavy industry. Its industrial base is solid, but ancient. The average Czech worker earns only $300 a month.

To compete on the open market, Czechoslovakia had to devalue its currency from nine korunas to the American dollar to 17 korunas to the dollar (for tourists, 38 to the dollar).

The difference between the rate of exchange for routine commerce (17:1) and that for tourists (38:1) is an interesting barometer of East European economics. A Czech citizen must work an entire month to earn 5,100 korunas (U.S. $300), but an American tourist can exchange U.S. $300 and get 11,400 korunas in return! The *tourist* then can stay in a hotel, buy a meal, ride a taxi, or purchase a souvenir for *half* of what it would cost a *local citizen!*

Of the remaining COMECON nations, three—Vietnam, Mongolia, and Cuba—are non-European nations and presumably will be left to fend for themselves.

Bulgaria is shackled by low productivity and shortages of food, yet in May 1990, it was announced that Club Med would open a resort on the Baltic Sea in this Eastern Bloc country.

Romania, a nation of 23 million people (roughly the same population as California) was the most hostile country in the Eastern Bloc toward the Kremlin, and the Romanian border with Russia is one of the tightest in the world.

Albania is probably the least receptive to foreign investment; because it is constitutionally forbidden to borrow abroad, it is pitifully poor.

Yugoslavia, a perennial hot-bed of ethnic differences, could very well split apart within the next few years. Economically, the country is in desperate shape. One can't even find a dry cleaner or a laundromat there.

Finally, the USSR

Perhaps the greatest shock of all has come with the collapse of the former USSR. Following unprecedented political unrest which included a brief military takeover and the house arrest of President Mikhail Gorbachev, the Soviet Union no longer exists. Three former republics, Estonia, Latvia, and Lithuania declared their independence on September 6, 1991. The republic of Georgia has also become independent. On December 21, 1991, the Commonwealth of Independent States was formed which includes the remaining 11 former USSR members:

Russia	Ukraine
Uzbek	Kazakh
Byelorussia	Azerbaijan
Moldavia	Tadzhik
Turkmen	Kirghiz
Armenia	

The Republic of Russia dominates this group and most others are expressing grave concerns about many issues including how power over military and nuclear weapons will be shared.

In the former USSR there are reportedly five million people unemployed and 30 million more who are not employed effectively and who probably should be fired. Much of the economy is a fabric of falsehoods, created by countless phony bookkeeping transfers. A typical worker earns 300 rubles per month, equal to $48 at the tourist's exchange rate (6.8:1) or $30 at a free market exchange rate (10:1). Of the 15 republics in the USSR, at least half of them are desperately seeking relief, even if it means going on their own.

Straightening Out a Mess

The Western nations have been actively working to assure that the economic revolution in the former Eastern Bloc and the USSR would succeed.

In January 1990, representatives of 34 countries met in Paris to form the European Bank for Reconstruction and Development in Eastern Europe. It represented the largest regional assistance effort since the Marshall Plan, and was modeled after the World Bank. At least $10 billion was assured for the purpose of providing loans, economic guidance, technical assistance, loan guarantees and, in some enterprises, equity investments.

On April 1, 1992, President Bush submitted to Congress an economic aid package for members of the former Soviet Union totaling $24 billion. Participation in funding will be shared by other Western nations who seem to have agreed that they have no choice but to help these faltering economies recover if there is to be any chance whatsoever for democracy to take root and survive.

"The changes in the former Soviet republics have created a defining moment in history," the president declared, warning that the cost of aiding those newly independent nations is "nothing like the price we would pay if democracy and reform failed."

By combining credit programs, repackaging previous pledges, and providing $6 billion to support the Russian ruble, the aid package is designed to help the painful reform of Russia's economy and encourage its move toward democracy.

The U.S. contribution of about $4.1 billion is roughly 17 percent of the total from Germany, Japan, Britain, France, Italy, Canada, and the U.S.

"The stakes are as high for us now as at any time in this century," Bush said.

The world's seven wealthiest industrialized nations will provide $6 billion to create a fund to stabilize the value of the Russian ruble, a key element in the economic reform program, and $18 billion in various other forms of economic aid from governments and international financial institutions.

The administration also said it would end outdated Cold War trade restrictions, enabling Russia and the other former Soviet republics to draw more on the resources of the Export-Import Bank and the Overseas Private Investment Corp.

Bush's proposal calls for an increased American presence in the independent republics through diplomatic missions, the Peace Corps, the U.S. Information Agency, and a new citizen democracy corps.

A major stumbling block is the lack of a sound currency and a workable rate of exchange for East European former Soviet currencies. PepsiCo, which has been doing well in Eastern Bloc countries for quite a few years, has had to export chairs from Poland to its Pizza Hut restaurant chain as a means of getting its profits out of Eastern Europe.

A second major problem is the condition of most European and Soviet factories, some of which are badly outdated. Many of those factories experience 20 percent more downtime than their Western counterparts because of a severe lack of spare parts.

Also, all of the Eastern and Soviet governments' bureaucracies will have to be restructured. Non-contributors will have to be removed. Some will have to be replaced. Virtually all will have to be retrained. Political turmoil will exist for quite some time and it is bound to hamper other efforts toward reconstruction.

But the East needs Western technology, capital and contacts. New coalitions will have to be formed based on trade opportunities. The East will have to open its markets and reschedule the payment of its debts.

Time To Get In The Game

The ones who move quickly will naturally be the ones to get the best deals, buy the best companies, arrange the best mergers, form the best joint ventures—at the best prices.

Probably the best entry to East European and Soviet markets is alliances in West Germany, Austria, Italy, France or Finland. In 1988, Western Europe exported $43 billion worth of goods to Russia and its satellites—ten times as much as the U.S. and 11 times as much as Japan.

The gross national product of East Germany, Hungary and Czechoslovakia combined is greater than China's. Eastern Europe constitutes the third largest home appliance market in the world. And East European workers are paid less than one-fourth of what West European workers are paid.

Eastern Europe's population is 30 percent larger than that of the EC. Combined, the two Europes (excluding the USSR) constitute a market of 600 million consumers.

Inefficient home markets in Eastern Europe provide many exceptional opportunities for American businesses. The Europeans are not accustomed to the entrepreneurial spirit or to taking risks. They need American managers—or, at least, American management skills—to compete in an open market.

But setting aside all of the unique opportunities to be found in Eastern Europe, which will be discussed individually and in some detail in later chapters, the value of establishing a foothold in Western Europe prior to December 31, 1992 cannot be over stressed. The EC, after all, is a $600 billion-a-year market!

The growth potential in the EC exceeds our own. America's economic growth in 1989 reached 2.9 percent; Europe's, 3.8 percent. Projections estimate that America's growth throughout the 1990s will be 2.5 percent per year; Europe's, over 3.5 percent. It only makes sense to compete in the most active markets available.

Gross Domestic Product

(in billions)

EC (including Finland)	$4,132
Eastern Europe	438
USSR	1,000
Far East (except mainland China)	900
Japan	2,400
U.S.	4,550

If the EC92 program is beneficial to Europeans, it also can be helpful to U.S. business. For example, it will now be necessary to file for patent, copyright, or trademark protection only *once*, rather than having to do so in each country. Another example: Perhaps you had been planning to buy or build a plant in West Germany (a very expensive country) and now, thanks to EC92, you are able to buy or build your plant in Ireland (a much less expensive country).

There are a number of other excellent reasons for entering the export market:

- Economy of scale;
- More efficient production and distribution;
- Reduced costs; and
- Larger profits margins

Another point to consider: in buying a company, merging with one or forming a joint venture, the price/earnings ratio of your potential partner is of considerable concern. Many countries throughout the world boast of companies with price/earnings ratios that have been comparable to ours. According to a report by Dean Witter Reynolds, Inc., price/earnings ratios over the period, 1980-89 have averaged as follows:

Price/Earnings Ratios

10-Year Average

France	17.4
Japan	33.9
The Netherlands	7.5
Norway	10.9
Spain	12.3
Switzerland	13.3
U.S.	11.7
West Germany	13.1

One should be aware that foreign accounting practices are not the same as ours. As a result, you may discover that your potential overseas partner has hidden assets and/or understated earnings that will make them a far more valuable ally than you originally believed.

A current American television commercial suggests that people should eat a particular brand of breakfast food because "it's the right thing to do." The same can be said for getting into the export market.

In 1988, a Dun & Bradstreet survey of 5,000 American companies disclosed that 11 percent of them planned to begin exporting in the following year. U.S. companies acquired a total of 185 European firms that year.

Outside of Europe, there are a great number of other exciting export opportunities. Japan, Korea, and Taiwan would seem to be particularly attractive markets in the Pacific because they have an expanding infrastructure and their demand for consumer goods is explosive.

Medium-sized companies appear to be in the best position to benefit from entering the export market. Small high-tech companies seem to be the ones who stand to lose the most by *not* starting to export. Many analysts believe that exporting will afford even more potential to those dealing in services than to those dealing in goods.

As the world's economic scenario unfolds, it seems certain that competition will stiffen and businesses of the future will have fewer but sharper competitors.

Certainly, expanding into the export market will enable you to attract new investors and make more effective use of your capital. Once a business has covered its fixed expenses, a hefty percentage of its income drops directly to the bottom line. Also, additional profits can be realized by taking advantage of favorable foreign currency exchange rates.

CHAPTER 2

IS EXPORT FOR YOU?

Since 1987, America has regained the lead as the world's top exporter, reaching a total of $364 billion worth of exports in 1989. But we also hold the lead as the world's top *importer* ($492.9 billion). If we are selling more abroad—and the figures show that we are selling 80 percent more in Canada and Europe, 90 percent more in Latin America, 100 percent more in Japan, and 130 percent more in Asia's newly developed countries than we were in 1983—we also are *buying* more from our offshore competitors.

It is important to realize that 95 percent of the world's population—the world's consumers—live outside the U.S. Furthermore, that population is growing 70 percent faster than ours. This is a customer base that American businesses cannot afford to ignore.

One company that has learned how to handle the new global market as well as any is General Electric Co., America's largest diversified industrial firm. GE sees its most profitable markets overseas and is doing something about it.

With 40 percent of its $5.7 billion in operating profits coming from abroad in 1989, and pretax income growing at an annual rate of 30 percent overseas compared to half that rate in America, GE has realized that its fastest-growing and most profitable markets are offshore. It also has realized that some drastic steps have to be taken to strengthen its position in some of those markets.

First, it absorbed Monogram's and RCA's appliance businesses, merging them into its own GE and Hotpoint lines. Then it entered into a joint venture with Britain's General Electric Co. (not related), England's largest appliance manufacturer. As a result, one out of four home appliances purchased anywhere in the world today is a GE.

Other corporations have made similar strides in their own fields and in their own ways:

Abbott Labs:	Exports up 25.2 percent
Boeing:	Exports up 40.4 percent
Caterpillar:	Exports up 35 percent
GE:	Exports up 26.5 percent
IBM:	Exports up 11 percent
Merck:	Exports up 39.3 percent
Motorola:	Exports up 35 percent
Rockwell International:	Exports up 29 percent
Tenneco:	Exports up 28.8 percent
Xerox:	Exports up 93 percent

McDonald's has 8,289 restaurants in the United States, but it also has 2,916 restaurants overseas: *Toys 'R' Us* opened 25 European outlets during the past five years and is now penetrating Malaysia. Three-quarters of Coca-Cola's profits come from outside the U.S. IBM does 54 percent of its business overseas. Eli Lilly gets 40 percent of its pretax income offshore.

All of this is well and good for the corporate "generals"—General Motors, General Electric, General Mills, General Dynamics—but few companies are in their league. What about the companies that only rank as "buck privates" or "corporals" in the business hierarchy?

Surprisingly, perhaps, the small-to-medium-size firms as a class are doing better than their larger cousins in the international sector. Indeed, the U.S. Department of Commerce says most of the growth in our GNP is coming from export—and smaller businesses get most of the credit. Only 15 percent of the companies in America are involved in export, but of those companies, *78 percent have fewer than 100 employees!*

According to New York's National Institute of Business Management, 46 percent of the nation's small- to medium-sized businesses were engaged in export in 1986, but in 1987, *73 percent* were involved.

Small companies have several advantages over their larger counterparts:

- They usually are more flexible.

- They have a shorter chain of command.

- They can offer more personalized service—a big asset in many overseas markets.

- They can make decisions and act on them more quickly.

Some examples?

Home Industries of Cedartown, GA manufactures agricultural equipment. Annual sales are around $12 million—all of which come from overseas.

Hettinga Equipment of Clive, IA makes plastic molding machinery and employs about 100 people. Three-fourths of its revenues come from foreign markets.

Preco Industries of Lenexa, KS spent two and one-half years nailing down its first Japanese contract. Now, over 20 percent of the company's $7 million in sales comes from export.

Tracom, a Ft. Worth, TX company that sells used diesel engines, is four years old, has 14 employees and does about $3 million a year in sales. Forty percent of its revenues come from export.

Menlo Tool of Warren, MI sells $3 million worth of special cutting tools a year. Twelve percent of its sales come from Europe.

Bilco Tools of Houma, LA sells $2 million worth of oil field equipment each year. About one-third of its sales come from overseas.

Cenogenics Corp. of Morganville, NJ makes a variety of diagnostic test products for the medical field. In 1989, the 25-employee company was doing business in 36 countries. Those overseas customers were producing 58 percent of the company's sales, and president Michael Katz was named National Small Business Exporter of the year by the U.S. Small Business Administration.

Where Do You Fit In?

So how do you determine when, where, and how to take your company into the export business?

Obviously, you don't make a move of that magnitude without a reason, but there are a great many excellent reasons for getting into the export market:

- Increase overall sales volume
- Enlarge sales base to spread out fixed costs
- Use excess production capacity
- Compensate for seasonal fluctuations in domestic sales
- Find new markets for products with declining U.S. sales
- Exploit existing advantages in untapped markets
- Take advantage of high-volume foreign purchases
- Learn about advanced technical methods used abroad
- Follow domestic competitors who are selling overseas
- Acquire knowledge about international competition
- Test opportunities for overseas licensing or production
- Contribute to the company's general expansion
- Improve overall return on investment
- Create more jobs

As you give some thought to entering the export market, be sure your domestic operation is strong. Do not over-tax your company by taking on more than you can handle.

Is Export for You? 21

If business is bad at the moment, wait for it to turn around before you think about going international. On top of the other problems to be faced during a business lull, an attempt to begin exporting could be the final straw.

Can you envision an export market for your company that can generate 15 percent or more of your annual sales? That is the level that many experts consider to be a sound starting point. At this juncture, however, you probably don't know; you'll need to do a little market research.

Many companies prefer to hire an outside agency that specializes in this type of research, but with some time and effort, you can do the job yourself. Here is what you need to find out:

- What is the largest market(s) for your product?
- What is the fastest-growing market(s) for your product?
- Are there any trends that you should be aware of?
- What is the market outlook?
- What are the current conditions and practices in the market?
- Who are your competitors?
- Specifically, what products must you compete against?

Put some time, money, and effort into analyzing your export potential. Avoid optimism and attempt to be as realistic and as objective as possible. Be cautious and learn as much as you can. Contact your industry trade organizations. Study American and foreign trade journals. Talk to appropriate state and federal agencies involved in your field and/or international trade in general. Talk to those who have personal knowledge of the countries with which you hope to do business. Talk to experts at your local college or university.

Start by screening your potential markets. Obtain export statistics that show what products have been shipped to what countries by referring to:

Embassies (for their national trade statistics)

22 Chapter 2

Organization for Economic Cooperation & Development (OECD), United Nations

U.S. Department of Commerce

Export Statistics Profiles analyze reports for a specific industry, product-by-product, country-by-country, for the previous five-year period. Includes an *Export Market Brief*, which highlights the industry's prospects, performance and leading products. Available for 35 industries. Price: $70 each.

Custom Statistical Service has data on products not covered by an *Export Statistics Profile*. Will tailor the data to your needs. Price: $50 to $1,000 or more.

Foreign Trade Report, FT 410 is a monthly publication that itemizes shipments from the U.S. to foreign countries. Include quantities and dollar amounts for the month and year-to-date. Price: $9.50 per issue or $100 for a year's subscription, but also available in many libraries and in U.S. and Foreign Commercial Service District offices. To buy, contact Superintendent of Documents, U.S. Government Printing Office, Washington, D.C. 20402, phone (202) 783-3238.

Annual Worldwide Industry Reviews include country-by-country market evaluations, export trends, and five-year statistical tables of U.S. exports for a single industry. Price depends on the industry involved: $200 for one volume, $350 for the two volumes or $500 for three volumes.

U.S. Small Business Administration

Export Information System Data Reports cover about 1,700 product categories, the 25 largest markets for the product, the 10 best overseas markets for a U.S. exporter of the product, market trends, and chief sources of foreign competition. No charge.

Now pick out the five or ten largest and fastest-growing markets for your product. Has market growth been consistent from year to year? If there was a period of economic recession, did the import growth continue or resume as soon as the economy recovered?

Pick out some smaller but fast-emerging markets in which you may be able to get in on the ground floor. Look for particularly high growth rates.

Now, target three, four, or five of the markets that seem to offer the best potential and concentrate your attention on them. Examine not only the prospects for your product(s), but for any products that could influence a demand for your product. Look at overall consumption and compare that to the amount being imported. Refer once again to the *Export Statistics Profiles* and the *Annual Worldwide Industry Reviews*, as well as the Census Bureau's *World Population* and the U.N.'s *Statistical Yearbook*, which contain a great deal of demographic information. Also available from the U.S. Department of Commerce and potentially helpful:

> *International Market Research* reports provide an in-depth analysis of one industry in one country. Includes market size, market outlook, end-user analysis, distribution channels, cultural characteristics, business customs, business practices, competitive analysis, trade barriers and trade contacts. Price: $50 to $200.
>
> *Country Market Surveys* are eight- to 12-page summaries of International Market Research reports. They highlight market size, trends and prospects. Price: $10 per country.
>
> *Country Trade Statistics* gives data on all U.S. exports to one country over a five-year period. Shows the leading and fastest-growing U.S. exports to that country. Price: $25 per country... with a discount for ordering reports on multiple countries.

Study your competition. Are there local companies in the field? What other foreign countries will you have to compete against? Check *International Market Research* and *Country Market Surveys*. What is the U.S. market share?

Using the same publications, check the factors that will affect your marketing efforts. Are there any factors, such as cultural peculiarities or unfamiliar business practices, that will influence the use of your product? Are there any U.S. barriers, such as export controls, that would prevent you from exporting to your targeted country? Any foreign barriers, tariff or non-tariff? Does the U.S. or the targeted country offer any incentives to encourage your export?

Don't try to do too much at the outset. Concentrate on your best prospects and expand slowly from there.

Now that you have as much information as possible, go into the field and look things over for yourself. Visit the targeted country and concentrate particularly on observing the things that will affect your business—wholesale channels, transportation, retail practices, competitive practices, user habits and preferences.

Attend some international trade shows. Pick up as much competitive literature as you can. Ask probing questions of the sales representatives staffing their booths.

Participate in an industry- or government-sponsored trade mission. Talk to potential suppliers, distributors and customers. Get some opinions from people whose views you respect.

If you fail to engage in the world market, an overseas manufacturer may seize the opportunity and produce a "copycat" version of your product. A solid export program will not only guard against this sort of thing but it will discourage overseas competitors from attacking your home market.

Be sure you can answer all of the following questions:

Researching Your Export Potential

A. Experience

    1. What countries have we already done business with?
    2. What countries have we received inquiries from?
    3. What product lines are mentioned most frequently?
    4. Have we been doing more business abroad lately?
    5. Have we been getting more inquiries from abroad lately?
    6. Who are our main domestic competitors?
    7. Who are our main foreign competitors?

B. Management and Personnel

    1. Who will be responsible for the export departments' organization and staff?
    2. How much senior management time should be allotted to export?
    3. What are my expectations from export?
    4. What organizational structure is needed for the export operation?
    5. Will this move cause any internal political problems?
    6. Who will follow through from planning to implementation?

C. Production capacity

    1. How is our present capacity being used?
    2. Will it hurt domestic orders to handle our export business?
    3. Will we need additional production? How much? What will it cost?
    4. Are there fluctuations in our annual workload? When? Why? will export production help the situation or worsen it?
    5. What minimum order quantity should be required?
    6. Will we have to redesign our product for export? What will it cost? How long will it take?
    7. Will we need new packaging for the export market? What will it cost?

D. Financial capacity

    1. What amount of capital can we afford to tie up in export?
    2. What start-up budget will we need? Can we afford it?
    3. What on-going budget will be required? Can we afford it?
    4. Will our export effort conflict with anything else we are planning to do?

5. By what date must our export activity become financially self-sustaining?
6. How are continuing costs to be allocated between the domestic operation and our export activity?

If the prospect of export still looks appealing, the next thing you will need to do is develop an export strategy. You will have to adopt an international point of view. Accounts receivable probably will go up, for example, because there usually is more merchandise in the pipeline. Some of your employees may have be to be shuffled around. Some will have to shoulder new (possibly additional) responsibilities. Some may even have to be let go.

Your overseas pricing will have to be studied to reflect the additional costs associated with export.

Outlining Your Export Strategy

Table of Contents
    One- or two-page executive summary

Introduction
    Why a company should export

Part I: Export policy commitment statement

Part II: Statement of the company's position
    Product
    Operations
    Personnel and export organization
    Resources of the firm
    Industry structure
    Competition
    Demand

Part III: The Marketing Component
    Identification, evaluation, and selection of target markets
    Product selection and pricing
    Distribution method

Terms and conditions regarding export sales
Internal organization and procedures
Sales goals
Profit (loss) forecasts

Part IV: Tactics
Countries where firm enjoys special advantages, such as family ties
Primary target countries
Secondary target countries
Indirect marketing efforts

Part V: The Export Budget
Pro forma financial statements

Part VI: Implementation Schedule
Follow-up
Period operational/management review

Addenda
Basic market statistics—historical and projected
Background facts
Competitive environment

Planning an export strategy deserves as much attention as you would devote to your domestic planning. After years of practice, domestic planning may have become more or less routine, but haphazard consideration of a strategy that will move your company into the international market could lead to serious errors.

The Most Common Mistakes

The most common mistakes made by new exporters, says the U.S. Department of Commerce, are:

- Failing to obtain qualified export counseling.
- Failing to develop a master marketing strategy.
- Inadequate commitment from management.

- Too little care in selecting overseas distributors.
- Chasing helter-skelter around the world instead of establishing a firm plan for profitable and orderly growth.
- Neglecting the export business during market booms at home.
- Failing to treat foreign and domestic distributors alike.
- Presuming that one product and one marketing approach will be successful in every country.
- Failing to modify the product to satisfy the market's regulations or cultural preferences.
- Failing to print service, sale, and warranty documents in the local language.
- Failing to consider associating with an export management company.
- Failing to consider licensing or joint venture possibilities.
- Failing to provide readily available product servicing.

Basis for Success

Conversely, the companies that have enjoyed the greatest success in export have demonstrated:

- Product excellence
- Marketing excellence
- The desire to get an early start
- Patience in expanding the business incrementally
- A strong commitment from management

Be Flexible

Whatever your strategy, be flexible. When doing business on a global scale, you must continuously assess and revise your plans.

Do not expect to export in order to "see how it goes." Prepare for the long haul. Many companies find that it takes four or five years to develop a sound, profitable, smoothly functioning export operation.

Do not look to export for security or as a means of increasing your profit margins. Instead, look upon it as an opportunity for growth and as a way to establish business stability.

Do not look upon a particular country or region as a profit center. Instead, set up your product lines as profit centers. This will give you a much better—and more international—perspective on how your business is progressing.

If this is your first venture into export and you are less than confident about the strategies that you have in mind, you can test your plan against a computer simulation program developed for IBM PC computers and compatible systems. Called *Export to Win*, the program was developed for the Port Authority of New York and New Jersey by Strategic Management Group, Inc., and may be purchased for $99.95. (Contact Strategic Management Group, 3624 Market Street, University City Science Center, Philadelphia, PA, phone (215)387-4000.)

Before your export plan is implemented, you would be wise to consult *two* attorneys—the one you use in the U.S. and one in the country to which you plan to export. Laws are not the same throughout the world. Check into overseas taxes, customs inspections, product laws, transportation regulations, business practices and financial regulations. Protect your technology with patents and your trademarks with copyrights. Try to include non-compete clauses in all contracts.

Take advantage of the assistance that is available. Listen to your local allies, for example, when it comes to such matters as packaging, marketing and advertising. Look for the balance between your company's overall strategy and the local conditions that will determine how to carry it out.

Some additional rules of thumb:

- Low prices are seldom a substitute for good quality.
- Good, fast communication is essential.
- Good "team players" generally are the most successful.
- When developing literature in the local language, use a local to do it. Translators often produce stilted copy.

- Never think of export as a means of dumping surplus goods or outdated products.
- Seek markets in which your product can fill a critical niche.
- Resist the temptation to increase your prices. Try to establish a strong market share instead.
- The initial small orders you will receive probably will not be profitable.
- Watch your travel overhead; it can easily get out of line.

Some industries enjoy better export potential than others. Textiles, apparel, electronics and steel are not selling well at this time, but the aerospace, computer, oil field equipment, medical equipment, and chemical industries are currently competing quite well.

Selected Export Opportunities By Industry

Agricultural Products and Machinery

    Ghana   Israel
    Nigeria   Egypt
    Zimbabwe   Mexico

Aircraft and Aviation Equipment

    Sweden   Israel
    Singapore   Brazil
    Zimbabwe

Biotechnology

    Spain   Singapore
    Italy   Taiwan
    West Germany   Argentina

Communications

    Taiwan   Saudi Arabia
    Nigeria

Computers, Peripherals, and Software

France
Spain
Italy
United Kingdom
West Germany
Sweden
China
Hong Kong
Japan
Korea

Zimbabwe
India
Israel
Saudi Arabia
Egypt
Canada
Argentina
Caribbean Basin
Mexico

Consumer Household Products

Hong Kong
Japan

Canada
Mexico

Electricity and Power Generation

Nigeria
India
Egypt

Brazil
Mexico

Electronics and Components

France
Spain
Italy
United Kingdom
West Germany
Sweden
China
Hong Kong

Japan
Korea
Taiwan
India
Israel
Canada
Brazil
Mexico

Energy

France
Spain
Italy

Korea
Taiwan
India

Energy *(continued)*
> United Kingdom
> West Germany
> Turkey
> China
> Japan

> Egypt
> Canada
> Argentina
> Brazil

Food Processing Equipment
> France
> Korea
> Ghana
> Nigeria

> Egypt
> Argentina
> Caribbean Basin

Furniture and Supplies
> Hong Kong

Hotel and Restaurant Equipment
> Ghana

> Caribbean Basin

Industrial Process Controls
> France
> Spain
> Italy
> United Kingdom
> West Germany
> China
> Japan

> Korea
> Taiwan
> Israel
> Canada
> Brazil
> Mexico

Machine Tools
> Korea
> India
> Israel
> Canada

> Argentina
> Brazil
> Mexico

Is Export for You?   33

Medical Equipment
- France
- Italy
- West Germany
- Sweden
- China
- Hong Kong
- Japan
- Korea
- Taiwan
- India
- Saudi Arabia
- Canada
- Mexico

Mining Equipment
- Ghana
- Nigeria

Oil and Gas Field Machinery
- India
- Argentina
- Mexico

Paper and Paper Products
- China
- Hong Kong
- Japan
- Korea
- Singapore
- Nigeria
- Saudi Arabia
- Canada
- Caribbean Basin
- Mexico

Plastics
- China
- Hong Kong
- Korea
- Taiwan

Pollution Control Equipment
- Italy
- West Germany
- Korea
- Taiwan
- India
- Israel

Production and Testing Equipment for Electronics
- France
- United Kingdom
- West Germany
- Korea
- Taiwan
- India

Production and Testing Equipment for Electronics *(continued)*
    Sweden   Canada
    China   Brazil
    Japan   Mexico

Science and Analytical Equipment
    France   Korea
    Italy   Taiwan
    United Kingdom   Canada
    West Germany   Brazil
    China   Mexico
    Japan

Seafood and Fish Products
    France   Japan
    United Kingdom   Nigeria

Security and Safety Equipment
    Spain   United Kingdom
    Italy   Sweden

Sporting Goods and Recreation Equipment
    Sweden   Mexico
    Japan

Telecommunications
    France   Singapore
    Spain   Taiwan
    United Kingdom   India
    Turkey   Saudi Arabia
    Sweden   Canada
    China   Brazil
    Japan   Mexico
    Korea

Textiles, Apparel, and Textile Machinery
- France
- Italy
- United Kingdom
- West Germany
- Hong Kong
- Japan
- Korea
- Israel
- Saudi Arabia
- Canada
- Caribbean Basin
- Brazil

Transportation
- China
- Taiwan
- Nigeria
- Caribbean Basin

Vehicles, Auto Parts, and Accessories
- France
- United Kingdom
- West Germany
- Japan
- Korea
- Canada
- Caribbean Basin

Sometimes a product has to be revised. Most other countries have adopted the metric system, for example. This would cause you to switch to metric sizing for those countries.

Andrew Bohnengel of Perfect Measuring Tape, Toledo, OH also had to adjust to the metric system. Bohnengel sells disposable paper measuring tape to the Canadian textile industry, but when Canada went metric in the late 1970s, Perfect Measuring Tape had to follow suit.

A. T. Cross of Lincoln, RI sells $200 million worth of pens and pencils in 150 countries, but it hasn't always been easy. The product's slim lines did not appeal to the tastes of German men. The company had to develop a fountain pen for the European market—then discovered that it would sell well in America, too. In Thailand, Cross' ballpoints had to be modified to handle the high humidity. A major selling point: Cross pens carry a lifetime guarantee.

Even food products may require some adjustments. The Japanese have their own regulations for fumigating cherries, for example, but when a consortium of California shippers from the San Joaquin Valley met their specs, they quickly sold $4 million worth of fruit in Tokyo.

Electrical equipment must be able to operate on foreign voltages. Industrial equipment must satisfy local worker-safety regulations.

Plugs for electrical equipment come in a wide range of shapes in various countries. In order to offset that problem, one U.S. manufacturer ships its products abroad *without* plugs. They are attached once the products reach their market.

In reviewing your potential in a given market, be sure to see that it has set the technical standards for use within your industry, and be sure your products comply. In much of Europe, for example, the use of Teflon has not yet been approved. By 1992, Europe will have to set a code of uniform minimum daily requirements for vitamins. Because the U.S. has set standards for nearly everything, do not assume that other countries have or that, when they do, their standards will be anything like ours.

Since many Americans have given up smoking, the tobacco companies have looked to other markets, particularly offshore. In Japan, 60 percent of the people smoke; and in Thailand, 65 percent of the men over 20 years of age smoke. In Hong Kong, American cigarettes account for 70 percent of the market. But the Far East is not alone; in Uruguay, for example, 68 percent of the men and 32 percent of the women are smokers.

Occasionally, even the name of a product must be changed to suit offshore market conditions. Chevrolet was astonished to find that its Nova did not sell well in Mexico until it realized that *no va*, in Spanish, means "won't run." Coca-Cola had a similar language problem in Japan.

To be a successful exporter, you must determine how to make your product and your company stand above the crowd. One way, of course, is by producing a quality product. Quality is something over which you can exercise control.

Good research once again may be your best guide. Product specification requirements, such as electrical characteristics within a given market, can be found in Dun & Bradstreet's *Exporters Encyclopedia*. Another source of information regarding export opportunities is a Dutch newspaper called *Trade Channel*, available through American Business Communications, Tarrytown, NY, (914)631-1802.

Organizations such as the World Bank, the U.S. Agency for International Development, and the U.N. Development Program also can provide valuable information.

You Can Export Services, Too

Three-fourths of America's workforce toils in the service industries, yet today, service industry exports comprise just *one*-fourth of other exports.

Even in the manufacturing industries, from 65 to 75 percent of our workers perform service tasks. Indeed, services account for 75 percent of America's total business costs.

In 1987, the U.S. exported $58 billion worth of services—approximately one percent of our GNP. A year later, we exported $92 billion worth—about 30 percent of the world market for services.

U.S. Services - 1988 Profile

Industry	Exports	Imports	Differential
Education	$4.1 billion	$600 million	+ $3.5 billion
Telecommunications	2.4 billion	4.3 billion	- 1.9 billion
Professional Services	3.2 billion	1.6 billion	+1.6 billion
Financial Services	3.8 billion	1.7 billion	+2.1 billion
Travel	29.2 billion	32.1 billion	- 2.9 billion

A number of factors indicate a very favorable outlook for the American export of services:

- Many foreign companies are out-sourcing a variety of their service needs today.

- Like a runaway virus, franchises are capturing the fancy of foreign entrepreneurs.
- Services that are being marketed abroad frequently are based on a special body of knowledge, such as the computer software industry. The U.S. enjoys 67 percent of the world software market.
- The world market for services has grown at an average annual rate of 16 percent over the past decade. The market for goods has averaged a growth rate of about seven percent.

In 1985, American advertising agencies doing business abroad enjoyed $63.3 billion in billings. By 1989, their billings had more than doubled to $133.5 billion. American Express generates some 20 percent of its profits overseas. Federal Express, now serving nearly 100 countries, is racking up over $250 million a year in offshore sales. ServiceMaster negotiated 500 home cleaning franchises and was contracted to service 40 hospitals in Japan by 1987. Waste Management is hauling trash in such improbable places as Argentina, Australia, and Saudi Arabia.

The U.S. Department of Commerce says American businesses engaged in the following service industries can expect to find good opportunities overseas:

- Construction, Design and Engineering
- Banking and Financial Services
- Insurance
- Legal and Accounting Services
- Teaching Services
- Management Consulting Services

So do those engaged in health care and in computer software services, especially in the following countries:

Health Care
    Spain   Saudi Arabia
    West Germany   Egypt

Computer Software (in 1988, a $50 billion market)

France	Zimbabwe
Spain	India
Italy	Israel
United Kingdom	Saudi Arabia
West Germany	Egypt
Sweden	Canada
China	Argentina
Hong Kong	Caribbean Basin
Japan	Mexico
Korea	

Fifteen of the top 20 software companies in the world are American companies. We have a decided edge in that industry.

But as bright as the prospects may look for exporting your services, there are several unique problems associated with the export of services versus the export of hard goods:

- Intangibles are harder to sell. There is nothing to see, touch, taste or smell. Language differences create broader gulfs.
- Financing is more difficult to arrange. After all, there is nothing to repossess.
- It is difficult to establish standards for services.
- The sales of services is more personal. Once more, language and cultural differences create wider gaps between customer and supplier.
- Time often is of greater importance.

Perhaps these are some of the reasons why the U.N.'s General Agreement on Tariffs & Trade (GATT) has been ineffective in bringing about the type of international accord in services that it has in other exports.

Many countries provide little or no protection for intellectual property. The worst offenders are Argentina, Brazil, Egypt, India, Korea, Malaysia, Nigeria, China, the Philippines, Saudi Arabia, and Taiwan. In Argentina, for example, there are 24 copycats on the market competing against Pfizer's antiarthritic drug Feldene—and none of them pays Pfizer a royalty.

But the potential rewards offset the difficulties in most instances. Look for perspective markets by getting information made available by the Caribbean Development Bank, the Inter-American Development Bank, the U.N., the World Health Organization (WHO), and the World Bank.

If your field is construction, design, or engineering, contact the Engineering Division of the Export-Import Bank for leads at (202)566-8802.

The U.S. Department of Commerce has created the Office of Service Industries to assist companies wishing to export their services. Their phone number is (202)377-4781. Divisions of that agency handle specific industry groups:

Information Industries Division: (202)377-4781

Transportation, Tourism, and Marketing Division: (202)377-4581

Financial and Management Industries Division: (202)377-0339

An excellent advertising medium is *Commercial News USA*, a magazine produced by the Commerce Department's Worldwide Services Program and distributed to 200,000 agents, government officials, and other key parties overseas. A small fee is charged.

CHAPTER 3

SETTING UP YOUR BUSINESS FOR EXPORT

To this point, you have invested a great deal of time and energy in research. Do not be discouraged: it will pay off.

You have analyzed your products (or services) carefully. You have investigated the various overseas markets. You have determined that export can be profitable for you. And you have developed a business plan. If your organization needs a tune-up, this is the time to do it. Is the company financially sound? Is it functioning smoothly? Are you affiliated with a bank that has an international division?

A good bank can be invaluable. It can help you get credit information on foreign firms and overseas agents, help with the collection on foreign invoices, transfer money to other countries, exchange currencies, and finance exports.

Are you committed to stay for the long haul? If it took you two years to make your company profitable in the first place, it may take several times as long to make your export operations profitable.

Have you found a lawyer and an accountant with experience in foreign trade? Are your key people committed to this new opportunity? Have you attended a few foreign trade conferences or seminars? Gone on a trade mission? Have you taken advantage of all the help you can get? Have you been a participant, rather than merely an observer?

Have you focused on the reason(s) for exporting?

- To increase product revenues
- To develop your market position
- To tap into regional growth, such as that along the Pacific Rim

When responsibility is delegated, be sure to give it to those who are as enthusiastic about export as you are. Be sure that you agree on your key strategies. Train your people well and then give them your support.

Expect a few down turns. They happen. Establish a mechanism for resolving any conflicts that may arise among members of your staff, both domestic and international.

Exploring The Economics

Breaking into export will cost some money. No question about it. The smaller the company and the slimmer the resources, the more difficult the financial problems will be to resolve.

There will be travel expenses, promotional expenses and expenses associated with participation in trade shows and the like. Normal operating costs are likely to increase as well to cover:

- Material and labor needed to provide product for a new market;
- Added warehousing space at home and/or abroad to keep sufficient product in the pipeline; and
- Additional accounts receivable to tie up your available capital.

Even the cost of money may go up. It may be necessary to obtain financing to expand into overseas markets, enlarge production facilities, and so on. The more you need to borrow and the less tangible your collateral, the more costly that financing may be.

Funding exports requires higher overhead than handling domestic loans, so many banks avoid it—especially if the local borrower is new to the export business. Companies generally try to arrange a revolving line of credit, secured by their outstanding accounts receivable, but when the customers are overseas and out of reach, many banks are not eager to get involved. Overseas credit checks are difficult and expensive, and fluctuations in the value of the dollar make currency translations uncertain.

Fortunately, various types of assistance are available, both at the state level (see Chapter 8) and at the federal level (see Chapter 9).

Export-Import Bank Of The United States

Commonly known as Eximbank, this organization is an independent government agency that provides financial support for American exports. Smaller banks are often hesitant to loan money to finance sales to unknown buyers in little-known markets without the guarantees provided by Eximbank.

In 1983, Congress required Eximbank to guarantee lines of credit for small exporters for up to 10 percent of the bank's own funds.

The agency's *Export Credit Insurance Program* insures exporters against loss caused by a variety of political and/or commercial factors. The program is a cooperative effort, co-managed by the Foreign Credit Insurance Association, an association of private U.S. insurance companies. It:

- Protects exporters against the failure of foreign buyers to pay;
- Encourages exporters to offer foreign buyers competitive financial terms;
- Supports an exporter's penetration of high-risk foreign markets; and

Chapter 3

- Gives exporters and their local banks greater flexibility in handling foreign accounts receivable.

Foreign Credit Insurance Association offices include:

Northeast Regional Office
  40 Rector St., 11th Floor
  New York, NY 10006
  Phone (212)306-5255

Serves New England, New York, New Jersey, Pennsylvania, Delaware, Maryland, the District of Columbia, and Puerto Rico

Southeast Regional Office
  520 S. Omni International
  Atlanta, GA 30303
  Phone (404)522-2780

Serves Virginia, North Carolina, South Carolina, Georgia, Florida, Alabama, Mississippi, and Tennessee

Midwest Regional Office
  20 N. Clark St., Suite 910
  Chicago, IL 60602
  Phone (312)641-1915

Serves Ohio, Indiana, Michigan, Illinois, Wisconsin, Minnesota, North Dakota, South Dakota, Iowa, Missouri, Nebraska, Kansas, Kentucky, and West Virginia

Southwest Regional Office
  Texas Commerce Tower, Suite 2860
  Houston, TX 77002
  Phone (713)227-0987

Serves Texas, Louisiana, Oklahoma, Arkansas, and New Mexico

Western Regional Office
 Crocker Center
 333 S. Grand Ave., Suite 2580
 Los Angeles, CA 90071
 Phone (213)687-3890

Serves Alaska, Washington, Oregon, California, Hawaii, Idaho, Nevada, Arizona, Montana, Wyoming, Colorado, and Utah

With the FCIA, Eximbank offers a short-term insurance policy that is geared to the smaller, less-experienced exporter's needs. Regular insurance policies usually have a deductible provision for "first loss" commercial risk, but the Eximbank policy protects exporters against 95 percent of their commercial risk and 100 percent of their political risk. This protection, which is good for up to 180 days, is available to any company that had less than $1 million in export sales last year and less than $1.5 million in the past two years, and that has not used the services of Eximbank or FCIA during the past two years.

Another insurance program, introduced in 1984, is Eximbank's *Umbrella Policy*, which is available to exporters who have not been insured by FCIA during the previous two years and who have two-year export credit sales of $4 million or less.

Over 350 banks participate in Eximbank's *Commercial Bank Guarantee Program*, which requires the buyer to make a 15 percent down payment on its purchases and for the commercial bank to finance the remaining 85 percent. In the event of a loss due to commercial causes, 10 percent of it accrues to the exporter (except small businesses, as defined by the U.S. Small Business Administration, which are only assessed 5 percent); 5 to 15 percent accrues to the bank; and the rest is covered by Eximbank. Terms of repayment are:

Contract Value	Terms
Up to $50,000	181 days to 2 years
$50,000 - $100,000	Up to 3 years
$100,000 - $200,000	Up to 4 years
Over $200,000	Up to 5 years

Under Eximbank's *Small Business Credit Program*, an exporter's bank can provide foreign buyers with below-market, fixed-rate financing. The bank writes a fixed-rate promissory note for the borrower to sign and then borrows the unpaid balance of the note from Eximbank at one percent below its yield, as long as the interest rate on the note is not below the minimum rate set by Eximbank for the borrower's home country. This program is available to any small business, as defined by the U.S. Small Business Administration.

Another program, the *Working Capital Guarantee Program*, provides exporters with access to loans for working capital. Eximbank's guarantee covers only loans used for export-related activities. It covers 90 percent of the loan principal plus interest up to the stated rate of the loan, or one percent above the U.S. Treasury rate for comparable maturities up to the date of claim payment. Loans, which generally are for a period of one to 12 months, must be secured by an inventory of exportable goods, accounts receivable on goods or services already exported, or other suitable collateral of no less than 110 percent of the outstanding balance of the loan.

In 1984, Eximbank and the U.S. Small Business Administration created the *Working Capital Co-Guarantee Program* which combines Eximbank's Working Capital Guarantee Program and the SBA's Export Revolving Line of Credit Program. As a result, a small business may borrow up to $1 million for working capital using the resources of both agencies.

Also in 1984, Eximbank introduced the *Engineering Multiplier Program*, a lending program to help design, engineering, and architectural firms win contracts for foreign feasibility studies and for pre-construction design/engineering services. The contract must involve a project with the potential to generate additional U.S. exports worth $10 million or twice the amount of the initial contract, whichever is greater. Eximbank extends a medium-term direct loan to the foreign purchaser, amounting to 85 percent of the U.S. export value up to $10 million. The loan carries the lowest interest rate permitted under international guidelines. The buyer must make a 15 percent cash payment, and Eximbank will then guarantee commercial financing for the engineering company's costs in the host country of up to 15 percent of the U.S. export value. The maximum repayment period is five years, beginning six months after the contract completion date.

In 1988, Eximbank initiated a one-year pilot project called the *City-State Agency Cooperative Program*. Three cities—Columbus, OH; Los Angeles, CA and Tucson, AZ—and three states—California, Maryland and Massachusetts—were selected for the project, in which Eximbank provided specialists to guide businesses through the paperwork, while the cities and states provided the money and the professional services for the program.

In Arizona, the Tucson Local Development Corporation got $15,000 from the state and used that to leverage a $1.35 million line of bank credit, which it uses to provide export business loans of up to $100,000.

In California, the Los Angeles City Economic Development Office negotiated a $15 million line of credit with the Imperial Bank of Inglewood and established the L.A. EXPORT program. In addition to providing loans, for which borrowers pay a one percent fee to Eximbank for a guarantee or one percent premium, for credit insurance, L.A. EXPORT offers a full export counseling service for small- and medium-sized businesses.

Small businesses also may benefit from the frequent briefings held by Eximbank in Washington, D.C. These briefings include both group briefings and individual counseling sessions. For the dates of coming briefings, call (202)566-8990.

Overseas Private Investment Corporation

Overseas Private Investment Corporation is an independent, financially self-supporting corporation operated by the federal government and headquartered in Washington, D.C. It has two principal operating components, the Insurance Department and the Finance Department, which encourage and assist U.S. investors in less developed countries. The investments should offer potential benefits to the host country in the areas of job creation, skills training, import savings, export earnings or tax revenues, as well as assuring the U.S. expanded trade, employment, access to materials, and investor earnings. Such investments may include a U.S.

manufacturer's distributorship in a foreign country. OPIC-supported programs are now underway in more than 100 countries.

In all cases, a project must be commercially and financially sound. For financial assistance, the U.S. investor must have at least a 25 percent equity investment in the enterprise. There is no equity minimum to qualify for OPIC insurance protection. All projects must have the approval of the host country.

OPIC will loan companies with annual sales of less than $120 million from $100,000 to $6 million per project. It charges commercial rates for a period of seven to twelve years. It also guarantees bank loans of up to $50 million per project.

OPIC will help finance feasibility studies by reimbursing 60 percent of the cost up to $100,000. For studying the economic and market conditions that a proposed project would encounter, a company may be reimbursed for overseas living expenses of about $100 a day, a fee allowance or salary of about $250 and economy-class air fare.

A separate OPIC program reimburses small businesses (annual sales under $120 million) for travel costs up to $5,000 for visiting a foreign country to explore business opportunities.

OPIC's long-term insurance (12 to 20 years) protects against currency inconvertibility, expropriation or takeover, and physical damage due to war, revolution, or civil strife.

Typical OPIC Insurance Rates

(1988)

Coverage	Base Rate Per $100
Inconvertibility	.30
Expropriation	.60
War, Revolution, Insurrection	.60
Civil Strife Rider	.15

OPIC also conducts investment missions to foreign countries. Since 1975, over 40 countries have been visited and over 200 projects have been implemented. A typical mission will involve 15 to 25 companies and last from five to ten days.

Country Information Kits provided by OPIC contain information on economic and political conditions, trade laws, business customs and regulations, and investment incentives for some 100 countries. Contact OPIC at 1615 M St. NW, Washington, D.C. 20527; (202)457-7047 or toll-free (800)457-OPIC.

U.S. TRADE & DEVELOPMENT PROGRAM

This program provides loans that help American companies defray the cost of participating in foreign projects. Generally, these involve major projects involving a country's infrastructure—roads, bridges, airports, and the like—but projects related to computer technology, medical technology, or education also may be involved.

This program has financed over 400 projects in 74 countries and produced over $800 million in U.S. exports since 1980. During the 1990s, its expects to generate some $7 billion in U.S. exports.

Trade & Development Program
10 Largest Beneficiaries
(FY 1981-87)

Country	$1,000s
China	15,711
Thailand	7,852
Philippines	4,631
Indonesia	4,298
Turkey	4,122
Colombia	3,956
Zimbabwe	3,910
Taiwan	2,374
Tunisia	2,347
Pakistan	1,676

In recent years, over half of the program's efforts have been directed toward Eastern Asia. Of prime consideration in approving any project is the likelihood that is will be completed.

Funds from the program are given to the foreign country, but with the stipulation that an American firm must be selected to conduct the study. The program will reimburse the company for half the cost of performing the feasibility study. A small business program also is available. For more information, call (703)875-4357.

U.S. Small Business Administration

Various SBA financial programs are administered through the agency's District Offices. These offices are listed in Chapter 8, and many of the SBA's programs are described there as well. Other SBA activities are described in Chapter 9.

The SBA provides loans and loan guarantees for equipment, facilities, materials, working capital, and specified export market development activities.

Of special interest is the *Export Revolving Line of Credit Program*. This program is available only to companies with headquarters in the U.S. and to companies that have been in business for more than a year, although the latter condition can be waived if the company's management warrants special consideration.

Requests for aid must come from your bank, and funds cannot be used to establish overseas joint ventures, to pay existing debts or to purchase fixed assets.

Small Business Innovation Research Grants

Under a program launched in 1982, the 11 largest federal agencies are required to set aside 1.25 percent of their external research and development budgets for companies that employ 500 people or fewer. During 1988, that tiny percentage provided $400 million in small business contracts. Each year, the 11 federal agencies involved in the program send out solicitations for Phase I grants (feasibility research). These grants run for six months and may amount to as much as $50,000. After the Phase I study has been completed, and if the results look promising, the company can apply for a Phase II grant, which can amount to as much as $500,000 over a period of two years. Following the Phase II grant, the company must get funding from private sources or from a regular government contract for commercialization.

Fewer than 15 percent of the applicants win a Phase I award, and only 40 percent of that number succeed in getting a Phase II grant. Still, the program provides seed money for high-risk, high-return, early-stage R&D—something generally out of the financial reach of small companies.

Over half of the companies that win a Phase I grant have fewer than 30 employees, and nearly half of the companies that win such grants have never had a previous grant.

Some states offer assistance in filling out the necessary applications for these grants. A few even offer additional funding to successful applicants.

This program is administered by the Small Business Administration, and additional information can be obtained by contacting them at (202)653-6458.

Commodity Credit Corporation

The Commodity Credit Corporation has an *Export Credit Guarantee Program* (GSM-102) designed to expand agricultural exports by encouraging U.S. banks to finance foreign purchases on terms of up to three years.

The foreign buyer's bank must issue an irrevocable letter of credit covering the port value (f.o.b. value) of the commodity. A Commodity Credit Corporation guarantee will cover most of the amount owed to the U.S. bank in case the foreign bank should default.

Countries barred by the Trade Act of 1974, barred by Executive Order, and barred by U.S. Department of Commerce regulations cannot legally participate in this program.

The program is administered by the U.S. Department of Agriculture. For added information on GSM-102, contact the Assistant

General Sales Manager, Export Credits, Foreign Agricultural Service, 14th St. & Independence Ave. S.W., Washington, D.C. 20250; (202)447-3224.

Other Financing Possibilities

When examining your options for financing, there are a number of considerations to bear in mind:

- Interest rates and financing fees vary. Be sure to consider the total cost of your financing as well as how that additional cost may affect the price of your product and its profitability.

- Long-term financing costs more than short-term financing. Use the length of term that is most advantageous to you.

- Be sure to check your customer's credit rating. High-risk sales will increase the cost of your financing and/or insurance.

- Do not seek outside financing if your company has the resources to handle its own or if it can establish a commercial line of credit.

- If you seek outside financing, weigh your possibilities carefully. Pick the source that is best tailored to your needs.

In addition to the sources already discussed, there are a number of other options. The International Trade Administration of the U.S. Department of Commerce has prepared a publication entitled *A Guide to Financing Exports* that may be helpful.

Large corporations like Sears and General Electric are forming their own export trading companies. They may prove to be an outlet for your product or service.

Companies known as "factors" or "factoring houses" buy a company's export receivables at a discounted price (possibly two to four percent below their face value). The discount will depend on the products involved, the customer's credit rating, and the country involved. Using a factor, you get immediate payment for your goods and avoid the problems of collection, but factors do business either with or without "recourse." If you use the services of a factor *with* recourse, you will be financially liable for the transaction if your customer defaults or if some other problem prevents payment within a reasonable period of time.

- The International Finance Corporation can underwrite capital stock subscriptions to provide financing for private firms that contribute to the welfare of an under-developed nation.

- The World Bank can guarantee loans to finance projects that benefit under-developed nations.

- The Inter-American Development Bank can guarantee loans for projects that lead to economic growth in Latin America.

- The Private Export Funding Corporation, with the approval of the Export-Import Bank, can lend money for short- to long-term periods to foreign importers that purchase U.S. goods.

None of these possibilities is a substitute for developing a strong relationship with your own bank, however. Such relationships may take some time to establish, but the long-range benefits are considerable.

How do you know you are affiliated with a bank that can serve your export needs most effectively?

1. How big is the bank's international department?

2. Does the bank have any foreign branches? Where are they?

3. Does the bank have any correspondent banks abroad? Where are they?

4. What does the bank charge for confirming a letter of credit? For processing drafts? For collecting payments?

5. Does the bank provide buyer credit reports? Is this service free or is there a fee? If a fee is charged, how much is it?

6. Does the bank have any experience with state and federal financing programs for small businesses?

7. What other export-related services does the bank provide?

An alternate to acquiring credit insurance of your own, for example, is to use your bank's master policy in order to protect your receivables. Is this service available at your bank?

Unfortunately, only a relatively small percentage of U.S. banks have international trade experience or care to provide it. Even the smallest bank will respond to the pressures of its customers, however, and if a number of business customers work together to force the issue, an interest in export financing will surely evolve.

The Goal Is Added Profit

During 1989, corporate profits earned in the U.S. declined by 19 percent. Profits earned abroad, on the other hand, *increased* by 14 percent.

Foreign sales can boost a company's earnings. Once the breakeven point has been reached, nearly all of the income drops straight to the bottom line.

When sales are made in a strong foreign currency, added profits result when that currency is converted into U.S. dollars.

Your competition is smart, and you will have to be smarter. You cannot allow yourself to become over-extended. You must strive to keep your costs down, but your quality up. The price of your product should cover your costs, your agent's commission (generally about six percent), and your other export costs.

You must price according to your competition, yet if you compete strictly on the basis of price, you can expect to find yourself limited to a few relatively unprofitable niches in the market.

CHAPTER 4

GET SET...GO!

TRADE SHOWS

The easiest means of getting started in export is to participate in a trade show. It is an easy and inexpensive means of obtaining information on competitors, potential agents, wholesalers, distributors and customers. With some luck, you may even receive a few orders and become engaged in the export business.

There are many ways to learn about suitable international trade shows:

- Study the trade journals, reading both the news pages and the ads.
- Contact your trade association.
- Write to any of the state and federal organizations (see Chapters 8 and 9).
- Subscribe to Business America, a biweekly magazine offered by the Superintendent of Documents, U.S. Government Printing Office, Washington, DC 20402-9325. Price: $49 a year.

The U.S. Department of Commerce is not only organized to provide assistance country-by-country, but industry-by-industry. All of the following telephone numbers should be prefaced with (202) 377-:

Industry	Phone
Aerospace	-8228
Automotive	-0823
Chemicals & Allied Products	-0128
Consumer Goods	-0337
Computers & Business Equipment	-0572
Energy	-1466
Products & Domestic Construction	-0384
General Industrial Machinery	-5455
Instrumentation	-5466
Medical Services	-0550
Major Projects & International Construction	-5225
Metals, Minerals, & Commodities	-0575
Microelectronics & Instrumentation	-2587
Services Industries	-3575
Special Industrial Machinery	-0902
Telecommunications	-4466
Textiles	-5078

D-O-C ITA also will help you to analyze foreign export statistics and trade data ((202)377-4211) and assist you if you need advice on export trading companies ((202)377-5131).

Do not go to an overseas trade show unprepared. This is the time to put your best foot forward. At home, you may be the big fish in a small pond, but offshore you will be judged against the best competition the world has to offer.

It may sound simplistic, but be sure to take plenty of product literature with you. Foreigners are notorious literature collectors. That way, they can cover ground quickly, study the literature at their leisure during the evening, and return to the exhibitor's booth the next day with questions.

Also, be sure that your literature is printed in the local language. If the trade show is held in England, you can be sure that those who attend it are proficient in English, whether they are Japanese,

French, German, or whatever. If the show is in Italy, on the other hand, you can assume that the participants will understand Italian, not necessarily English, so take literature printed in Italian.

When you have your product literature translated into Italian (or any other language), have the job done overseas. The high school language teacher may be handier and less expensive, but the translation probably will read like pidgin-English to a real Italian. Take the time to do the job right. A poor translation can be a turn-off to potential foreign customers.

If time is short or money tight, consider taking your normal literature (in English) *but using local-language inserts in it*. Be sure the inserts provide all of the vital product information, but also be sure they include the name, address, telephone number and fax number of your company.

Before you participate in a show, create a plan. What do you hope to accomplish? Selling 1,000 units of your product? Qualifying 50 leads to follow up later? Signing on four distributors? Whatever your objectives, write them down.

Do a little pre-show promotion. Send a personal invitation to attend the show to your key accounts and prime prospects. Followup by mail or with a telephone call. If complimentary show tickets are available, pass them along. Take out an ad in the key trade journal.

Select with great care the sales personnel that you want to staff your exhibit. Personnel who can speak and/or read the local language will be a definite help. Those who project a negative image *in any manner* could cause irreparable damage.

Once you have selected your staff, brief them fully and carefully. Make sure they are prepared for the conditions that they will encounter. The exhibition showroom is not the place to train your staff.

Be absolutely certain your exhibition staff knows everything there is to know about your products, pricing, delivery, financing, and so on. If a prospect has a question, he deserves to receive an answer. If he doesn't, you may very well lose his business.

Prepare a written staff schedule so that you and your staff will know exactly what they are to do throughout the show. Be reasonable and flexible.

Be sure your staff knows how to qualify leads and how to follow up once the show is over.

Devote some time to the design of your booth. Will it stop traffic? Stand out in the crowds? Deliver your message? Be remembered? Is it large enough—about 50 square feet for every salesperson on duty? Will it serve your product(s), your staff *and* your visitors? Have you provided ash trays, wastebaskets, seating, storage space?

Collect business cards from every serious prospect who stops in your booth. Follow up on each one after the show is over.

Use your time at the show wisely. You may be wiser to study your competition or to sign up a distributor than to chase after every would-be customer. Your staff can work on the customer; but even so, be sure that they concentrate on the best prospects, not the easiest or most congenial. Go back to your list of objectives for being in the show to begin with, then proceed accordingly.

Trade shows are a great way to prospect for leads. When you consider that the average corporate sales call costs $280 these days, the cost of participating in top-quality trade shows seems very reasonable.

A great deal can be learned at trade shows. They can be much more than a convenient meeting place for manufacturers, suppliers, agents, distributors, dealers, and customers. Be alert to the more subtle opportunities. Does your product meet foreign safety standards? Would a slight modification in your product make it more marketable (or more profitable) abroad? How does your product compare to its competitors? How do the people at the show respond to your product? What do they say about it? Do they like your packaging?

Participating in overseas trade shows may not be without occasional customs problems. Other countries do not want us to take our products there for exhibition and/or demonstration and then sell them to avoid paying duties or taxes on them. To avoid this concern, you may wish to obtain a carnet (pronounced car-nay), a bond or credit letter that assures the payment of duties or taxes on any product(s) not taken back home. Carnets may be obtained from the International Chamber of Commerce, 1212 Avenue of the Americas, New York, NY, 10036; (212)354-4480.

A fee is charged for a carnet according to the value of the merchandise that is covered. A bond, letter of credit or bank guaranty amounting to 40 percent of the value of the goods also is required, thereby securing the duties or taxes in question. A carnet generally is valid for one year.

Catalogs

Another means of gaining exposure for your company and its product(s) abroad is through the distribution of your product catalog.

Frequently, major trade shows will feature an area in which such catalogs are put on display. In other situations, it may be possible to have a supplier, customer, or some other business ally put out your catalog in *their* exhibition booth. In still other situations, notably conferences and seminars at which there are no formal product exhibitions, *only* the manufacturers' catalogs are offered to participants.

Not to be overlooked, either, are the services of the U.S. Department of Commerce, which will see that your catalog is offered through the worldwide network of U.S. Embassies, at a cost of $90 per country.

Once again, go to the trouble of having your literature translated for the market(s) you hope to reach. This is not to say that you must be prepared to produce a special edition for every country, just every major language. Your basic English edition, for example, will serve your needs in England and in Canada. A Spanish edition not only serves your interests in Spain, but in Central and South America, and several other Spanish-speaking regions of the world.

Select A Suitable Bank

If you intend to engage in international trade you will need a bank that has the services and experience to handle the sort of financial affairs involved.

You will need to arrange for an international letter of credit, an instrument that will enable you to arrange business deals far more easily, quickly and (probably) profitably than if you were not to have one.

You will need to transfer dollars into yen, marks, pounds and other forms of foreign currency and vice versa. It may become necessary to track exchange rate fluctuations on a daily basis.

It will be helpful to have a means of checking on the credit of various business associates.

For your convenience, American banks involved in world trade are listed alphabetically by city.

Alabama
    American National Bank & Trust Co.
    First National Bank of Mobile
    Merchants National Bank of Mobile

Arizona
    First National Bank of Arizona
    Valley National Bank

California
    Beverly Hills National Bank
    Banco Nacional de Mexico, S.A.
    Bank of America N.T. & S.A. International Banking Office
    First Western Bank & Trust Co.
    The Hong Kong of California
    Security Pacific National Bank
    Central Valley National Bank
    First National Bank of San Diego
    United States National Bank
    American Trust Co.
    Bank of America
    Bank of California
    The Barclay Group of Banks
    Crocker-Citizens National Bank
    First Western Bank & Trust Co.
    Sumitomo Bank of Calif.
    United California Bank
    Wells Fargo Bank

Colorado
    First National Bank of Denver
    Denver United States National Bank

Connecticut
    Connecticut National Bank
    City Trust Co.
    Hartford National Bank & Trust Co.

Florida
    Atlantic National Bank of Jacksonville
    Barnett National Bank
    Florida First National Bank
    Central Bank & Trust Co.
    The First National Bank of Miami
    Pan American Bank of Miami
    First National Bank
    Exchange National Bank of Tampa
    Marine Bank & Trust Co.

Georgia
    First National Bank of Atlanta
    Citizens & Southern National Bank
    The Trust Company of Georgia
    Savannah Bank & Trust Co.
    Liberty National Bank

Illinois
    American National Bank & Trust
    Continental Illinois National Bank & Trust Co. of Chicago
    Exchange National Bank
    First National Bank of Chicago
    Harris Trust & Saving Bank
    LaSalle National Bank
    Northern Trust Co.

Indiana
    American Fletcher National Bank & Trust Co.
    Indiana National Bank

Get Set...Go! 61

Kentucky
   Citizen Fidelity Bank & Trust
   First National Bank
   Liberty National Bank

Louisiana
   The National Bank of Commerce
      in New Orleans
   Whitney National Bank of
      New Orleans

Maryland
   Equitable Trust Co.
   First National Bank
   Maryland National Bank
   Mercantile Safe Deposit &
      Trust Co.
   Union Trust Company of
      Maryland

Massachusetts
   The First National Bank of Boston
   The National Shawmut Bank
      of Boston
   New England Merchants
      National Bank
   State Street Bank & Trust Co.
   South Shore National Bank
   Mechanics National Bank of
      Vancouver
   Third National Bank of Hampden
      County
   Valley Bank and Trust Co.
   Safe Deposit Bank and Trust Co.

Michigan
   Bank of the Commonwealth
   The Detroit Bank & Trust Co.
   Manufacturers National Bank of
      Detroit
   National Bank of Detroit

Minnesota
   Duluth National Bank
   National Bank of Commerce
   First National Bank

   Northwestern National Bank
   First National Bank of St. Paul

Missouri
   Commerce Trust Co.
   First National Bank
   United Missouri Bank
   First National Bank in St. Louis

New Hampshire
   Merchant's National Bank

New Jersey
   Bank of Commerce
   Fidelity Union & Trust Co.
   First National State Bank
   Bank of Commerce
   Fidelity Union Trust
   First National State
   Hudson Trust Co.
   First National Bank of
      Passaic County

New York
   Manufacturers & Traders Trust
   Liberty National Bank
   Marine Midland Bank West
   American Express Co.
   Atlantic Bank of New York
   Bank of America International
   Bank of China
   Banca Commerciale Italiana
   Banca Nazional del Lavoro
   Banco do Brasil s.a.
   Banco De Ponce
   Banco di Napoli
   Banco di Roma
   Banco Nacional de Mexico
   Bank of China, N.Y. Agency
   Bank of Indonesia
   Bank Leumi li-Israel B.M.
   Bank of London & South
      America, Ltd.
   Bank of Japan
   Bank of Montreal
   Bank of Tokyo Ltd.

Chapter 4

New York, continued
  The Bank of Nova Scotia
  The Bank of Tokyo Trust Co.
  Bankers Trust Co.
  Barclays Bank Ltd., London
  Canadian Bank of Commerce
    Trust Co.
  Canadian Imperial Bank of
    Commerce
  Chase Manhattan Bank
  Chemical Bank New York
    Trust Co.
  Credito Italiano
  Cai-ichi Bank Ltd.
  Federal Reserve Bank
  Fiduciary Trust Co. of New York
  The First of Boston Int'l Corp.
  First National City Bank
  French American Banking Corp.
  Fuji Bank Ltd., The
  Israel Discount Bank
  Irving Trust Company
  Industrial Bank of Japan
  Lloyds Bank Limited, London
  Manufacturers Hanover Trust Co.
  International Divison
  Marine Midland Trust Co. of N.Y.
  Merchants Bank of New York, The
  Mitsui Bank Ltd.
  Mitsubishi Bank
  Morgan Guaranty Trust Co.
    of N.Y.
  National Bank of North America
  Nippon Kango Bank Ltd.
  Overseas Disount Corp., Inc.
  Philippine National Bank
  The Royal Bank of Canada
  J. Henry Schroeder Banking Corp.
  Standard Chartered Bank Ltd.
  Sterling National Bank
  Sumitomo Bank Ltd.
  Swiss Bank Corp.
  Swiss Credit Bank
  Toronto-Dominion Bank
  Security National Bank of L.I.
  The Standard Bank Ltd.
  State Street Bank

  Tokai Bank Ltd., The
  United States Trust Co. of New
    York
  Wells Fargo Bank

North Carolina
  North Carolina National Bank
  First National Bank of
    North Carolina
  Bank of North Carolina
  First Union National Bank
  Wachovia Bank & Trust
  Wachovia Bank & Trust Co.

Ohio
  First National Bank of Akron
  The Central Trust Co.
  Fifth-third Bank
  The First National Bank of
    Cincinnati
  Society National Bank
  The Cleveland Trust Co.
  The National City Bank
    of Cleveland
  Union Bank of Commerce
  City National Bank & Trust
  Huntington National Bank
  Ohio National Bank
  The First National Bank
  Third National Bank
  The Toledo Trust Co.
  The National Bank of Toledo

Oklahoma
  First National Bank & Trust

Oregon
  The First National Bank of Oregon
  The Oregon Bank
  United States National Bank

Pennsylvania
  Central-Penn National Bank of
    Philadelphia
  First Pennsylvania Banking
    & Trust Co.

Pennsylvania continued
  The Fidelity Bank
  Girard Trust Co.
  The Philadelphia National Bank
  Provident National Bank Equibank NA
  Mellon National Bank & Trust
  Pittsburgh National Bank

Puerto Rico
  Banco Credito
  Banco De Ponce
  Banco Popular de Puerto Rico

Rhode Island
  Industrial National Bank of Providence
  Rhode Island Hospital Trust Co.

Tennessee
  First National Bank
  Union Planters National Bank

Texas
  American National Bank
  First Security National Bank
  First National Bank
  Pan American Bank
  National Bank of Commerce
  First National Bank in Dallas
  Mercantile National Bank at Dallas
  Republic National Bank of Dallas
  State National Bank
  Southwest National Bank
  First National Bank
  Moody National Bank
  United States National Bank
  First City National Bank of Houston
  Bank of Southwest/National Association
  Texas National Bank of Commerce

Utah
  Walker Bank & Trust

Virginia
  Bankers Trust of S.C.
  South Carolina National Bank
  Bank of Virginia
  Virginia National Bank
  First and Merchants National Bank of Richmond

Washington
  Pacific National Bank
  Peoples National Bank of Washington
  Rainier National Bank
  Seattle-First National Bank

Washington D.C.
  American Security & Trust Co.
  Riggs National Bank of Washington

Wisconsin
  First Wisconsin National Bank
  Marshall & Ilsley Bank
  Marine National Exchange Bank

Setting Up An Office

Everything about a business takes on a different dimension once it becomes involved in export. All of these things are associated with the growth in size and sophistication that a business needs to experience. Most of the changes are exciting, challenging, and even *fun*.

First—and perhaps most obvious—is to designate someone or some group to be in charge of international business. Give them all the authority they will need. Do not make the mistake of treating them any different—neither better nor worse—than their domestic counterparts.

A useful machine is the telex, which is both faster and less expensive than the telegram or cable. Of major importance is the fact that the telex gives you a permanent "hard" copy, which the telephone does not. You can lease (for roughly $50 a month) or buy (for about $1,100) your own telex machine, or you can sign up with a commercial telex service. A third possibility involves installing a personal computer, modem, printer, and the appropriate telecommunications software, then signing up with a service like Western Union's "Easylink" or MCI's "Mail," which charge you nothing but the cost of a local phone call to receive a message and only the transmission charge to send one. An added benefit to the latter approach is that the modem-connected personal computer also can be used to tap into various databases that will provide you with information on a wide range of useful topics.

Also, look into the possibility of installing a fax (facsimile) machine. These high-speed, low-cost devices are quickly replacing the telex. A photocopy of an actual document is sent and received via fax, and a fax operator does not have to "type in" the material, thereby creating a totally new document, causing more work, and creating an additional opportunity for errors. Many overseas customers, particularly those who are not adept in English, feel a lot more comfortable with a formal document than some form of verbal communication.

You will be using the telephone differently now. Check with your long-distance carrier regarding the various services that are available, and weigh them to determine which service will be most useful to your business. As of December 1989, for example, AT&T offered customers toll-free calls from Mexico and 40 other countries over regular telephone lines. MCI offered similar service to 15 countries. U.S. Sprint offered such service only to Canada, but was expanding into other countries. Under the AT&T plan, customers are charged $20, a fee for the actual telephone time used, and a one-time start-up fee of $43.50 for service to one country and $99 to each additional country.

AT&T offers another potentially useful service called USADIRECT. With it, someone overseas can dial a number and be connected with an AT&T operator in the States who then will complete the call.

When you decide to enter the export field, it is a good time to review the manner in which your company is organized. If it is not already incorporated, this may be a good time to do so. You may even elect to establish your international operations as a separate corporation. Investigate the advantages and disadvantages of every option.

One important consideration is whether or not your company has or will have facilities overseas. If it does (or will), "stock pairing" may be something to look into. Under this option, a foreign company in which five or fewer American shareholders own 50 percent of the stock or more may be considered an American corporation and hence subject to the payment of about 50 percent in corporate taxes on the profits. If the company has more than five shareholders none of whom owns a controlling interest in the business, it could set up its foreign operations as a separate corporation established in some tax-free nation like the Cayman Islands. Stock is issued in the new corporation on a share-for-share basis and distributed to the parent company's shareholders as a dividend. As long as the two companies function separately, both legally and operationally, the parent company avoids the U.S. corporate income tax and only the dividends paid to the shareholders are taxable as personal income.

Be absolutely certain that your product is fully protected in the international marketplace. Laws regarding patent and copyright vary widely from country to country. Some developing nations have made it a practice to pirate another country's products and then flood the world market with inexpensive look-alikes.

Within the U.S., such matters are supervised by the U.S. Patent and Trademark Office, Washington, D.C. 20231; (703)557-3158, which produces the following useful booklets on the subject:

- *Patents and Inventions: An Informal Aid for Investors*
- *Questions and Answers About Patents*

Chapter 4

- *Attorneys and Agents Registered for Practice before the U.S. Patent Office*
- *Official Gazette of the U.S. Patent Office*
- *General Information Concerning Patents*

The U.S. Small business Administration, P.O. Box 15434, Ft. Worth, TX 76119 also has two helpful publications:

- *Introduction to Patents* (MA 6.005); and
- *New Product Ideas* (SBB90)

Whether considering the legal reorganization of your company or the security of its products abroad, the services of a good lawyer—and perhaps a tax accountant—are invaluable. Either one should be knowledgeable and experienced in handling international trade matters.

There are a number of other matters that should be investigated while you are organizing your office and staff:

- The negotiation of contracts
- Restrictions on the payment of bills with U.S. currency
- Obtaining the approval of foreign governments for contracts
- How to handle corrupt officials abroad
- How to deal with a lack of cooperation, particularly in critical government offices abroad
- Obtaining entry or work visas for U.S. personnel to foreign countries
- Dealing with restrictions on the repatriation of profits
- Handling social welfare costs and worker protection laws in foreign countries
- Necessary product modifications such as electric power differences and metric differences
- Advertising prohibitions

The U.S. Small Business Administration has created the Management Assistance Division to help you deal with problems such as these. Many of their programs are described in Chapter 9. Also of potential value is their network of Small Business Development Centers, which are based upon the expertise of personnel associated with various universities. These individuals also should be able to counsel you.

You'll Probably Need A License

Violations of the Export Administration Regulations carry both civil and criminal penalties. Do not operate on guesswork or hunches. If in doubt, ask an official source . . . and get the answer in writing. Contact the Office of Export Administration, U.S. Department of Commerce, Room 2091, Washington, DC 20230; (202)377-4266.

For reasons of national security, foreign policy, or a shortage of certain domestic products, the government regulates the export of all goods and technology through the use of export licenses. These are issued for specific *transactions*, not to companies or individuals, and are of two types:

- A *general* license is a broad grant of authority to all exporters for certain categories of products. Individual exporters do not need to apply for these.

- A *validated* license is a specific grant of authority to a particular exporter for a particular product. These are issued case by case, either for a specified period of time or for a single transaction.

To determine which license you need, you will need to go through three steps:

1. Check the schedule of country groups in *Export Administration Regulations* (15 CFR Part 370, Suppl. No. 1). Into what group does the country to which you are shipping your product fall?

68 Chapter 4

2. Check the Commodity Control List (15 CFR Section 399.1 Suppl. No. 1). Does your product require a validated license for shipment to that country group?

3. Determine if any "special restrictions" apply.

To avoid any problems, contact the Department of Commerce Exporter Assistance Division, Room 1099D, Washington, D.C. 20230; (202)377-4811.

This process has now been automated. A system called ELAIN (Export License Application and Information Network) operates 24 hours a day, seven days a week. For information, call (202)377-8540.

If you think your export license has gotten tied up somewhere, you can check that by telephone, too. STELA (System for Tracking Export License Applications) can be contacted using a push-button phone. Call (202)377-2752 and wait until STELA prompts you. Then enter your export license case number.

To ship under a *general* license, you must determine whether a Destination Control Statement is required. This statement appears on shipping documents to ensure that exports go only to legally authorized destinations. The commercial invoice and bill of lading displays a statement notifying the carrier and all foreign parties involved with the shipment that the material is licensed for export only to certain destinations and is not to be diverted contrary to U.S. law.

To obtain a *validated* license, the exporter must complete and submit an application (Form ITA-622P). A statement explaining the domestic use of the product and how the product will be used by the foreign purchaser should be included in a covering letter, as well as a statement as to whether the product can be altered for other uses. Technical manuals and specification sheets also should accompany the application, as well as a stamped, self-addressed postcard on the back of which is typed:

Date Received: _____
Case Number: _____

The postcard will be returned to you with the above information added so that you can refer to it if necessary.

Get Set...Go! 69

If the license application is approved, you will receive the license, which will include a number that must be inserted on the Shipper's Export Declaration (SED) form.

The exporter must record all shipments made under the license on the back of the license and then return the license to the Department of Commerce after it has been used or has expired. Be sure to keep a copy of all documentation. GET SERIOUS ABOUT MAKING CONTACTS.

By now, you should have been able to amass a sizeable list of contacts from:

- Participating in trade shows
- Responses to your advertising
- Suggestions from suppliers
- Recommendations from a variety of local, state, and federal resources
- Past and current customers
- Directories
- Old correspondence

Other sources of contacts may be available in your own locale. A complete listing of State contacts can be found in the Appendix.

Now is the time to begin contacting these sources in an earnest effort to increase your sales volume in each targeted market. As you do, you will begin to receive inquiries. These should be handled quickly—by air mail to minimize the response time.

Is your literature translated so that you can send your potential customer something he can use? Are your prepared to answer questions about delivery schedules, shipping costs and financial terms of purchase? What if a respondent wants to negotiate an exclusive arrangement in his region?

Do not be turned off by typing errors, poor spelling or letterhead that appears somewhat shabby.

When you reply, include information about your company. Stress your reliability as a supplier. Name prestigious customers. Provide bank references. Be polite, courteous and friendly, but not overly familiar. Avoid slang. If you make a promise, keep it. Avoid form letters—sign each letter personally. Establish a follow-up procedure and adhere to it religiously.

Producing your product plus the desired amount of profit is the "price floor" below which you should not go. The area between that point and the "price ceiling" established by market demand is the relevant price range within which you must work. Go above the ceiling and you will find no buyers; go below the floor and you will find buyers but will lose money.

When considering a pricing structure for an export market, one must realize that export entails additional cost—outlays over and above what it costs to produce and sell the product in the U.S. These costs include export documentation fees, ocean or air freight charges, insurance, the import duty, and the importer/distributor markup, which usually is higher than your domestic wholesaler's markup.

Less obvious are the additional costs of market research; credit checks; business travel; international postage, telephone and telex charges; translation fees; the training of foreign representatives; consultant, international attorney, and accountant fees; product modifications; and special packaging.

Modifying your product to suit export requirements may result in a savings, rather than an expense, and the added sales produced abroad may reduce your production costs on a per unit basis. Still, when the extra costs are added in, you may find that your product is no longer price-competitive when priced according to the cost-plus method.

A more realistic pricing technique may be the "marginal cost" method of pricing, which considers the direct out-of-pocket expenses of producing and selling export products as a floor beneath which the price cannot go. In addition to the production costs, overhead, and R&D, other costs should be allocated to domestic and export products according to the benefit that each derives from those expenditures. Once the actual cost of the product has been established, then the consumer price in the export market can be calculated.

The company's export market objectives should also be taken into account. Are you exporting in order to find a market for surplus production or an outmoded product? Or are you looking for long-term growth, increasing market share, a future springboard for new product introductions?

The quotation should describe the product, state the price of the product *at a specified delivery point*, set the time of shipment and specify the terms of payment. It also should indicate the gross and net shipping weight of the order and the total cubic volume and dimensions when packed for shipping. It is advisable to quote the price in U.S. dollars to avoid problems with fluctuating foreign exchange rates. If applicable, any trade discount should be shown. Any insurance and shipping charges should be shown, as well as the total charges to be paid by the customer.

Any additional terms and conditions should be clearly spelled out. The following statement is considered something of a standard for that purpose:

Sample Quote Form

Prices quoted herein are firm for _____(days, weeks, months) after _____ 19___. Delivery date will be quoted upon receipt of an order. Delivery of (product) can be made to shipside ____ days after receipt of order and receipt of a confirmed letter of credit. Terms of payment to our company: An irrevocable confirmed letter of credit issued by your bank and irrevocably confirmed by your bank's U.S. correspondent bank, or by our bank, __ _____. The prices covered in this quotation are in terms of currency of seller's country and are subject to change without notice unless exception is indicated. All orders received and accepted by us are contingent upon the acceptance of the order by the supplier, and deliveries are subject to delays caused by strikes, floods, fires, riots, the contingencies of transportation, unavoidable accidents, acts of God, or any other causes of delay beyond our control. Orders accepted by us are not subject to cancellation. Any taxes or consular fees imposed by any government authority on the sale of this order and not shown shall be paid by the buyer. All CIF quotations subject to present freight and insurance rates.

CREDIT CHECKS

Checking the credit of an overseas buyer is essential. Leave nothing to chance where the question of full and prompt payment is concerned.

You may ask the prospective customer for credit references, such as from the bank with which he does business. Check out these references in full. Your bank or its overseas affiliate may do this for you. Various credit-rating services are available. Your overseas agent or distributor might be able to handle it for you. For a fee of $65, the U.S. Department of Commerce will give you a report on any foreign firm, although such a report may take as long as two months to prepare. Whatever methods you use, be sure it is accurate, current, and thorough. Then act accordingly.

Remember that a bad credit rating does not mean the loss of a prospective customer. It may mean, instead, that you should ask for payment in advance, rather than offer 60 days' credit. Always:

- Select a safe method of payment, the safest being a confirmed, irrevocable letter of credit.
- Acquire credit risk insurance.

If a payment problem does arise, resolution of the problem can be difficult, time-consuming, and costly. Even when you have credit risk insurance, the insurer will insist that you exhaust all reasonable means of obtaining payment before your claim will be honored. Even then, a significant delay may occur.

As a first recourse, try arbitration. The International Chamber of Commerce ((212)354-4480) provides this service, as does the American Arbitration Association ((212)484-4000).

Sometimes, the U.S. government's trade compliance service will help, but only as a means of reestablishing communication between the disputing parties.

Get Set...Go! 73

Figure 4.1 Application for Export License

FORM DIB-628 (REV. 3-75)	U.S. DEPARTMENT OF COMMERCE DOMESTIC AND INTERNATIONAL BUSINESS ADMINISTRATION BUREAU OF EAST-WEST TRADE OFFICE OF EXPORT ADMINISTRATION	Not approved unless the official validation stamp appears hereon.	LICENSE NUMBER
EXPORT LICENSE		VALIDATION	

License is hereby granted to the licensee named herein, upon the terms and provisions stated herein, to export from the United States the articles, materials, technical data, or supplies herein described. This license is granted in reliance on representations heretofore made by the licensee to obtain it and is expressly subject to all export control laws, regulations, rules, and orders. It is not transferable without written permission from the Office of Export Administration.

1. LICENSEE	2. PURCHASER
3. ULTIMATE CONSIGNEE IN FOREIGN COUNTRY	4. INTERMEDIATE CONSIGNEE
5. COUNTRY OF ULTIMATE DESTINATION	6. APPLICANT'S REFERENCE NO.

QUANTITY	DESCRIPTION OF COMMODITIES	EXPORT CONTROL COMMODITY NUMBER AND PROCESSING NUMBER	UNIT PRICE	TOTAL PRICE
				TOTAL

NOTE:

- An Export License must be returned immediately to the Office of Export Administration, Room 1617M, Domestic and International Business Administration, U. S. Department of Commerce, Washington, D.C. 20230, (a) when it has been fully used, (b) when it has expired, or (c) when it has been determined that it will not be used or will no longer be used.
- Each shipment made against this license shall be entered on the reverse and licensee must sign prior to returning it.
- A Destination Control Statement is required to be shown on all bills of lading, air waybills, and commercial invoices. (See Export Administration Regulations § 386.6.)

Figure 4.1 Application for Export License *(continued)*

CHAPTER 5

MANAGING THE BUSINESS

Having entered the world market, you now must master the ins and outs of finance, shipping, documentation requirements, and customs regulations. While experience truly is the best teacher, we will attempt to get you started in the right direction.

Pricing, Quotes, And Setting Terms

If you are to make a profit from your export activities, you must price your product properly, provide complete and accurate quotations, and offer a suitable selection of terms.

Your price, of course, is determined by your costs, the competition, and the market demand. Also to be considered is your long-term objective, since you may be more willing to sell for less if you are anxious to establish your presence in a new market than if you are taking a more short-sighted view.

Pricing decisions should be made market-by-market since there is a great deal of difference between, for example, a major economic

Chapter 5

power and a Third World nation, or between a market with intense competition and one that has none.

Pricing And Costs

Overseas, as here, the demand for a product is a key factor in establishing prices. If the per capita income in a country is so low that it barely covers the cost of life's essentials, then a luxury item or an impulse item cannot be expected to find much of a market.

As a businessperson, you already know that many companies are prone to price their products by the "cost-plus" method, which begins with the manufacturing cost and then adds a figure to compensate for administration, overhead, R&D, shipping, distributor margins, customs charges, and profit.

Cost-Plus Method

	Domestic Sale	Export Sale
Factory Price	$15.00	$15.00
Domestic Freight	1.40	1.40
	$16.40	$16.40
Export Documentation		1.00
		$17.40
Ocean Freight and Insurance		2.40
		$19.20
Import Duty (12% of landed cost)		2.38
		$22.18
Wholesaler Markup (15%)	2.46	
	$18.86	
Importer/Distributor Markup (22%)		4.88
		$27.06
Retail Markup (50%)	9.44	13.54
Final Consumer Price	$28.30	$40.60

Obviously, this system pushes the consumer price to a rather high level—one that may not be attractive to the consumer or be competitive with similar products on the market.

A more realistic approach to pricing for the overseas market may be the "marginal cost" method. Using this technique, *the direct, out-of-pocket expenses* of producing and selling an export product are used as a base below which prices cannot be profitably set. In more understandable terms, domestic and export products are *not* costed-out equally. If the export product is a stripped-down version of the domestic model, the production cost should be less. If added production for export does not increase your fixed costs (labor, machinery, plant space), their unit cost should be lower.

Also, under the marginal cost method, such things as advertising and R&D are allocated between domestic products and export products *in proportion to the benefit derived from them*. Therefore, little or no U.S. advertising expense would be factored into the price of the export product, nor would any R&D expense if you were simply selling an established product to a new market.

Not all of the benefits associated with this technique accrue to the export item. If, for example, the domestic price suffers somewhat by having to "pay the freight" for all of the R&D, the export price suffers in kind by having to absorb the costs exclusively related to export, such as:

Market research
Business travel
International telephone, postage, and cable charges
Translation
Credit checks
Overseas commissions
Overseas training costs
Consultants
Freight forwarders
Special packaging
Product modification

Granted, the cost-plus system may be easier, but the marginal cost system may make your product a lot more competitive overseas—and give you a better perspective as to what your costs are and where the money is going as well.

Competition

If you have a new or unique product, you will be able to avoid competitive pressures—at least for a time. For the most part, however, competition plays a large role in setting prices.

Having an established market share, a well-known brand name, and quality product enable you to keep your price high. Entering a new market, with an unknown brand and unproven quality make that very difficult. Study the market, study the competition, and adjust your price accordingly.

Market Demand

For better or worse, we live in a world of haves and have nots. Everyone wants more; often, the "have nots" can't afford it. As obvious as it may seem, this can be a powerful factor in determining what products will sell and what will not in a specific market.

In some countries, the necessities of life are hard to come by. To offer those people some expensive and utterly impractical "impulse" item is bad business. True, there are those who succeed in selling refrigerators to the Eskimos and Gucci shoes to the Nigerians, but that is not the way to establish a successful export business. Whenever possible, look beyond what people *want* and determine what they *need*.

Quotations

Having determined your pricing strategy, you are in a position to answer the inquiries that your contacts are beginning to produce. Sooner or later, each potential buyer is going to ask for a quotation or a *pro forma* invoice, which is not an invoice for payment but a sample which the buyer can use when arranging for funds or applying for an import license.

Take great care in preparing a price quotation. Double-check all of your calculations. Make it clear that it is a firm, fixed quotation, but that it is valid only for a specific period of time. State that the shipping date will remain open until the order is received.

Many export sales begin with a request for a quotation or a pro forma invoice. A quotation should describe the product, state a price *at a specified delivery point*, specify the time of shipment, and state the terms of payment. It should include:

- the buyer's name and address;
- buyer's date of inquiry and reference number;
- list of requested products and a description of each;
- an indication whether the item(s) is new or used;
- price of each item (stated in U.S. dollars);
- gross and net shipping weight (probably in metric terms);
- cubic volume and dimensions packed for export (probably in metric terms);
- trade discount, if any;
- delivery point;
- insurance and shipping costs;
- period during which the quotation is valid;
- total charges to be paid by customer;
- estimated shipping date to customer or (preferably) to U.S. port; and
- estimated date of shipment's arrival.

Often, a pro forma invoice is requested with or instead of a quotation. This is not an invoice for payment but a "sample" invoice—or quotation in invoice format.

In addition to the information contained on a quotation, a pro forma invoice should carry a declaration that the invoice is true and correct and a statement citing the goods' country of origin. It also should be conspicuously marked pro forma invoice.

When you submit a quotation, be absolutely sure to state that it is subject to change without notice. If you agree to or guarantee a specific price, be sure to specify the exact time period during which that offer will remain valid.

Terms Of Sale

In arranging an export sale, it is very important to have the terms of delivery *and* the terms of payment clearly understood by all parties to the transaction. Terms that are common here may not be as common overseas. Similarly, similar-sounding terms may cause costly misunderstandings.

Some of the terms commonly used in export trade are:

Cost, Insurance, Freight (CIF)
Cost and Freight (C&F)
Free Alongside a Ship at the Named U.S. Port of Export (FAS)
Free on Board (FOB)
FOB Named Inland Point of Origin
FOB Named Port of Exportation
FOB Vessel (at Named Port of Export)
EX (Named Point of Origin)

These and other terms are defined in the Glossary at the end of this book.

Be sure to use terms that will be meaningful to your customer. "FOB Burlington, Iowa, not export packed" will be senseless to most people abroad. They would not be able to determine important, but unspecified costs, so they probably would not place an order with you.

Whenever possible, quote CIF because that tells your prospective buyer what it will cost to get the merchandise to a port somewhere near him. An international freight forwarder will help you with this, usually at no cost.

Packaging And Shipping

Packaging is important to your export program, and that means the immediate package as well as the bulk container.

Whether your product is bagged, bottled or boxed, important legal and consumer information should be considered.

- Are international brand names important to the sale of your product? Would a private label, tailored to local tastes and preferences, help the product sell better?

- Are the colors used on your package offensive to people in the country you are entering? Many cultures identify colors with death, their flag, or some other meaning.

- Should your label be translated into the local language? Some laws require it.

- If required by law, does your label or package contain information regarding product content or country of origin?

- Are weights and measures stated in local units (for example, liters instead of quarts)?

- Have you reviewed your packaging through the eyes of your consumer? The picture of a cardinal might appeal to Americans, but a peacock might be more attractive to Asians; the Stars and Stripes to an American, the Rising Sun to a Japanese.

- Must each item be separately labelled?

Establishing a brand name can be costly. Your ability to safeguard a brand name varies from country to country. In some countries, there are barriers to the use of foreign brand names and trademarks, while in others, counterfeiting and piracy are common. If a question exists, consult a local adviser or attorney.

When it comes to the bulk container in which you pack your merchandise for shipment, you must take the following into account:

- Breakage

- Weight

- Moisture

- Pilferage

Apart from the rough handling your shipment will encounter here, a shipment going by ocean freight may be loaded onto a vessel by a sling, in a net, by conveyor, by chute, or by some other method. In the hold of the vessel, other goods may be stacked or dropped on it. Overseas, it may be dragged, pushed, rolled, or dropped during unloading, while passing through customs or while en route to its final destination. Chances are it will be handled many more times—by whatever means—than your typical domestic shipment. The prevention of breakage is the shipper's responsibility.

Shipping charges are almost exclusively based on weight, thus you do not want to add to your costs by using a shipping container that weighs more than necessary.

Moisture is a major problem, particularly when products are shipped by sea or sent to certain parts of the world where high humidity and frequent rains are common. The shipment may sit on an open dock during transit. Some places do not have covered storage depots. You can combat moisture by shrink-wrapping your shipment or by adding material to your package that will absorb moisture.

Theft may occur at any unguarded moment. The stronger the shipping container, the less vulnerable you are. Not mentioning the contents or brand names on the package will discourage pilferage. Strapping, shrink-wrap and seals also help to prevent theft.

Often, your buyer will specify what packing is to be used. In any event, you should:

- Pack in a strong container, suitably filled and sealed.

- Be sure the weight is evenly distributed within the container.

- If possible, pack the goods on pallets.

- Use moisture-resistant material for both the packages and the packing filler.

Some carriers and private leasing companies offer special shipping containers. The more familiar are semi-truck trailers that lift off their wheels at the time of shipment and are placed atop another set of wheels once they reach their destination. These usually are best suited to packages of a standard size and shape.

Shipping by air generally requires less heavy-duty packing than ocean shipments. In most cases, your usual domestic packing procedures will suffice. Where an extra measure of protection seems advisable, tri-wall boxes or high-test cardboard (250 pounds per square inch or more) should be adequate.

Both carriers and insurers will be able to give you sound advice.

Marketing

There are four principle reasons why various types of labeling are used in export shipping: to satisfy shipping regulations, to assure proper handling, to conceal the nature of the contents, and to help the receiver identify the shipment.

Usually the overseas buyer will specify what export marks are to be used for easy identification.

Exporters need to include the following on containers that they ship:

- The shipper's mark
- Country of origin (USA)
- Gross weight (in pounds and in kilograms)

- Net weight (in pounds and in kilograms)
- Number of packages—size of case (in inches and in centimeters)
- Handling marks (international picture-symbols)
- Cautionary markings (i.e., "Use No Hooks" or "This Side Up"— both in English and in the language of the destination country)
- Port of entry
- Hazardous material warnings (universal symbols established by the Inter-Governmental Maritime Consultative Organization)

Markings should be legible, stenciled in waterproof ink and on three sides of the container. Any previous markings should be obliterated.

If more than one package is being shipped, indicate the number of packages in the shipment.

"Blind" marks, used to conceal the contents of boxes containing expensive merchandise, should be changed frequently.

Ports of the World, a free publication produced by CIGNA insurance, P.O. Box 7728, Philadelphia, PA 19101, should be helpful.

Freight Forwarders

An international freight forwarder acts as your agent in moving cargo to its overseas destination. They can be of particular value to a company that is new to export or that is too small to have its own international shipping department.

Freight forwarders are familiar with foreign countries' import regulations, U.S. export regulations, methods of shipping and all of the necessary documentation that is required. They can provide you with the information needed to prepare a price quotation. They can advise you on how to pack your shipment and arrange to have it contained. They can review your documentation to see that everything is in order and reserve space for your shipment aboard an ocean vessel.

Forwarders are paid a fee of about $125 for handling sea freight and about $50 for handling air freight, but these fees vary and are subject to negotiation. They also receive a commission of 1.25 to 10 percent from the carrier.

You will find forwarders listed in the yellow pages and in some trade journals. Search for one who:

- Has an office near the port(s) or airport(s) from which you will be shipping
- Has experience in handling your kind of cargo
- Is familiar with the destinations to which you will be shipping
- Has friendly, competent personnel
- Has a good credit rating

You will tell your forwarder what is to be done with your shipment by preparing a *letter of instructions*. This is exactly what you would suppose it to be—a letter containing such information on what you are shipping, to whom, whether or not to prepay the freight, how much insurance (if any) to acquire, and how to handle the documentation.

Financial Matters

Having received an order and shipped the merchandise, it is time to get paid. Of course, these details should have been worked out well in advance, but a variety of procedures are common in international trade. The most common are:

- Cash-in-advance
- Open account
- Consignment
- Letter of credit
- Documentary drafts for collection

Cash-in-advance is the most favorable arrangement for the seller, but the one most likely to create trouble for the buyer. As a result, unless buyer and seller have a well-established relationship, the amount of the order is small, or some other mitigating factor is involved, another type of payment may be preferable.

Open accounts can be as risky for the seller as cash-in-advance is for the buyer. Furthermore, they tie up his funds until payment is received. Again, this manner of payment usually is reserved for good customers of long standing.

Consignment is another "iffy" proposition. The exporter sends merchandise to an overseas agent who attempts to sell it. If the merchandise is sold, the proceeds—less the agent's commission or fee—are remitted to the exporter. During the interim, however, the exporter's merchandise (funds) are tied up, out of his control, and subject to every vagary from currency fluctuations, fire, and flood to theft or bankruptcy—and even revolution. Anyone engaging in this method of marketing is well advised to check his agent's credit carefully and take out adequate property risk insurance.

More commonly, *letters of credit* or *documentary drafts* are used in international trade. The former are relatively simple, positioning a responsible third party (generally a bank) between buyer and seller to assure that the one gets his merchandise as ordered and the other receives the agreed-upon payment. Documentary drafts are like checks but with conditions.

In the first case, the seller and the buyer agree on the terms of a sale. The buyer then arranges for his bank to open an irrevocable *letter of credit*, which will contain instructions concerning the shipment for the seller. The letter is sent to a U.S. bank with a request for confirmation.

The U.S. bank prepares a letter of confirmation and sends it, plus the letter of credit, to the seller. Assuming there are no problems such as the inability to meet the shipping date (in which case the buyer should be notified immediately), the seller has the merchandise sent to the appropriate port or airport by the freight forwarder. This done, the forwarder completes the necessary documents, which he or the seller will then send to the U.S. bank as evidence that their end of the transaction has been fulfilled.

The bank will review the documents and, if they are in order, issue the seller a check. It then will airmail the documents to the buyer's bank, which will review them and send them on to the buyer so that he or his agent can claim the shipment.

A bank will not pay more than the amount specified in the letter of credit, even if higher shipping charges, insurance, or other fees have been documented. A letter of credit should immediately be compared to the terms of the pro forma quotation to assure conformity. If any information in the letter is incorrect, absent, or even misspelled, the seller should immediately contact the buyer to ask for an amendment to the letter of credit.

The most common problems that arise when letters of credit are involved include:

- Late shipment
- Late presentation of the documents
- Improperly signed documents
- Undated documents

Documentary drafts are used in several ways. The buyer pays a local bank for the merchandise and then receives the documents required to obtain the goods. A draft that calls for payment before the goods are received is called a *sight* draft. A draft that calls for payment within a specified period after the goods have been received (such as 60 days) is called a *time* draft. A draft that calls for payment on a specific date (such as June 11) is called a *date* draft.

Foreign Exchange

Whenever possible it is to the exporter's benefit to give quotations and request payment in U.S. dollars. That way he knows exactly where he stands.

The dollar fluctuates in value compared to that of foreign currency. If an exporter agrees to sell some merchandise to a French buyer for 500,000 French francs at a time when the franc is worth $.20, he expects to receive $100,000 for the shipment. But, if the value of the franc slips a penny to $.19 before the transaction has been completed, the exporter will receive only $95,000—a $5,000 loss. Of course, it is possible that the franc might *gain* one cent in value, in which case the exporter would get a $5,000 bonus, but generally speaking, exporters do not prefer to gamble on the international money market—a separate business entirely.

Currency fluctuations can delay payment unless the terms of the sale clearly establish some limits. In the example above, for instance, a buyer who agreed to purchase goods with a $.20 franc will be in no hurry to pay a bill that is $5,000 higher than expected and will try to postpone payment until the rate of exchange is more favorable.

Not all foreign currencies are readily convertible into U.S. dollars. Should a situation arise where the buyer asks to make payment in a foreign currency, the exporter should consult an international bank before signing an agreement. Such banks can always offer good counsel, and sometimes will agree to purchase the foreign currency for a specified number of U.S. dollars, regardless of any fluctuations in the exchange rate. The bank will want a fee for this service, and that fee should be passed along to the buyer in the quotation or pro forma invoice.

Documentation

Export travels on its paperwork. Some 120 documents are used in international trade and, although the average is far less, as many as 70 documents may be required for one shipment.

Types of Documentation

Commercial Documents
    Terms and conditions of sale
    Contract
    Purchase order and acknowledgement
    Pro forma invoice
    Commercial invoice

Banking Documents
  Letter of credit application
  Letter of credit
  Advice of letter of credit
  Bank drafts

Transportation Documents
  Packing list
  Delivery instructions of domestic carrier
  Inland bill of lading
  Dock receipt
  Insurance request
  Insurance certificate
  Shipper's letter of instructions
  Ocean bill of lading
  Air waybill
  Booking request
  Freight bill
  Brokerage payment
  Forwarder's invoice
  Arrival notice
  Carrier's certificate and release order
  Delivery order
  Freight release

Government Control Documents
  Export license application
  Validated export license
  Certificate of origin
  Inspection report (from FDA, SGS, or other agency)

Consular invoice
Shipper's export declaration
Manifest (carrier to Customs)
Special Customs invoice
Customs entry

Insurance

Cargo insurance generally is acquired to safeguard against loss of damage in transit. Such insurance covers shipments by mail and air freight as well as by sea.

Depending on the terms of the sale, either the seller or the buyer may be responsible for obtaining the insurance. If the seller is responsible, the cost usually is added to the price of the shipment. The exporter may arrange for his own insurance or, for a fee, insure the cargo under the freight forwarder's policy. If a foreign buyer is responsible for obtaining the insurance, the exporter should require proof that this has been done for the adequate amount of coverage.

Standard insurance does not cover late arrival, rejection by governments or rejection by the buyers. Such coverage is available for a fee. Even all-risk insurance does not cover losses due to war, but a war risk clause usually can be added for a fee.

Generally speaking, small exporters tend to rely on their freight forwarder's insurance, while medium-sized exporters buy policies from insurance brokers. Large exporters will obtain an "open" policy that covers all shipments of normal merchandise within their normal trading area.

The insurance certificate generally is issued to the party that buys the insurance, but it is negotiable. Thus, if an exporter ships CIF to a customer and there is damage or loss, and the buyer must enter a claim, it is possible to do so.

Government Control Documents

All governments have a need to know what products are moving in and out of the country. The agency charged with this responsibility is called Customs.

Customs, however, does not operate independently. It simply sees to it that imports and exports conform to government specifications. In the U.S., food products, for example, must conform to regulations set forth by the Food and Drug Administration; meat and poultry, the Department of Agriculture; alcoholic beverages, the Bureau of Alcohol, Tobacco and Firearms; and so on.

Managing the Business   91

All export destinations except Canada are divided into country groups, according to the current status of relations between those countries and the U.S., existing trade agreements, and other relevant factors. The content of these groups changes periodically, so it would be impossible to present an up-to-date guide here. For the purpose of illustration, this was the list in the late 1980s:

Group Q	Romania
Group S	Southern Rhodesia
Group T	All Western Hemisphere countries except Cuba
Group W	Poland
Group Y	Albania, Bulgaria, Czechoslovakia, East Germany (including East Berlin), Estonia, Hungary, Latvia, Lithuania, Outer Mongolia, People's Republic of China, USSR
Group Z	North Korea, North Vietnam, South Vietnam, Cambodia, Cuba
Group V	All other countries except Canada

Policies regarding exports to these country groups are established to reflect current foreign policy. Restrictions on trade with Cuba (Group Z) have been in effect since 1960, for example. For a number of years, nonstrategic trade has been allowed with Communist countries in Country Group Y. As EC92 progresses, new U.S. policies will most likely be formulated.

To ensure that U.S. exports go only to legally-authorized destinations, a *destination control statement* is required on shipping documents. This notifies the carrier and all foreign parties that the merchandise in the shipment is licensed for export only to certain destinations and is not to be diverted contrary to U.S. law. Shipments to Canada and shipments made under certain general licenses usually are not subject to this requirement.

American policy opposes restrictive trade practices or boycotts imposed by a foreign country against any country friendly to the U.S. Anti-boycott regulations specifically:

- Prohibit a U.S. firm from refusing to do business with blacklisted companies and boycotted countries.

- Prohibit a U.S. firm from discriminating against another U.S. firm on the basis of race, religion, sex, or national origin in order to comply with a foreign boycott.

- Require public disclosure of requests to comply with foreign boycotts.

State and local regulations also are a factor in the movement of export and import. Generally speaking, however, they are of more concern to the importer and of little concern to the exporter.

The *certificate of origin* may be required to help prevent an importer from falsifying the country of origin and thereby pay a lower duty or bring in merchandise from a prohibited country. Such certificates usually can be obtained from a nearby chamber of commerce for about $15. The chamber certifies on the invoice that the merchandise was made in the U.S., and certified copies of that document become the certificates of origin. A product need not be totally composed of American-made parts to qualify for a U.S. certificate of origin; it qualifies if 35 percent of the product's value was added in the U.S.

Managing the Business   93

Figure 5.1 Statement by Ultimate Consignee and Purchaser

Figure 5.2 Bill of Lading

SHORT FORM BILL OF LADING
(Non-Negotiable Unless Consigned To Order)

NAME OF CARRIER

SHIPPER/EXPORTER (2) (COMPLETE NAME AND ADDRESS)

DOCUMENT NO. (5)

EXPORT REFERENCES (6)

CONSIGNEE (3) (COMPLETE NAME AND ADDRESS)

FORWARDING AGENT-REFERENCES (7) (COMPLETE NAME AND ADDRESS)

POINT AND COUNTRY OF ORIGIN (8)

NOTIFY PARTY (4) (COMPLETE NAME AND ADDRESS)

DOMESTIC ROUTING/EXPORT INSTRUCTIONS (9)

PIER/TERMINAL (10)

VESSEL (11) FLAG

PORT OF LOADING (12)

ONWARD INLAND ROUTING (15)

PORT OF DISCHARGE FROM VESSEL (13)

FOR TRANSSHIPMENT TO (14)

		PARTICULARS FURNISHED BY SHIPPER		
MARKS AND NUMBERS (16)	NO. OF PKGS. (17)	DESCRIPTION OF PACKAGES AND GOODS (18)	GROSS WEIGHT (19)	MEASUREMENT (20)

FREIGHT AND CHARGES PAYABLE AT

PREPAID ☐ **COLLECT** ☐

	PREPAID	COLLECT
TOTAL		

RECEIVED the goods or the containers, vans, trailers, pallet units or other packages said to contain goods herein mentioned, in apparent good order and condition, except as otherwise indicated, to be transported, delivered or transhipped as provided herein. All of the provisions written, printed or stamped on either side hereof are part of this bill of lading contract.

IN WITNESS WHEREOF, the Master or agent of said vessel has signed __________ bills of lading, all of the same tenor and date, one of which being accomplished, the others to stand void.

BY____________________
FOR THE MASTER

DATED

B/L NO.

Figure 5.3 Inspection Certificate

CUSTOMS FORM JUL 67 7512

Form Approved.
Budget Bureau No. 48-R212.7.

TRANSPORTATION ENTRY AND MANIFEST OF GOODS SUBJECT TO CUSTOMS INSPECTION AND PERMIT

BUREAU OF CUSTOMS

Entry No. ....
Port ....
Date ....

Entry No. ....
Class of Entry ....
(I. T.) (Wd. T.) (Wd. Ex.) (T. E.) (Drawback, etc.)

DIST. No. .... PORT CODE NO. .... FIRST U. S. PORT OF UNLADING ....

PORT OF .... DATE ....

Entered or imported by .... to be shipped

in bond via .... (C. H. L. number) .... (Vessel or carrier) .... (Car number and initial) .... (Pier or station) .... consigned to

District Director of Customs at .... (At customs port of exit or destination) Final foreign destination .... (For exportations only)

Consignee ....

Foreign port of lading .... B/L No. .... Date of sailing ....
(Above information to be furnished only when merchandise is imported by vessel)

Imported on the .... (Name of vessel or carrier and motive power) Flag .... on .... (Date imported) via .... (Last foreign port)

Exported from .... (Country) on .... (Date) Goods now at .... (Name of warehouse, station, pier, etc.)

Marks and Numbers of Packages	Description and Quantity of Merchandise Number and Kind of Packages (Describe fully as per shipping papers)	Gross Weight in Pounds	Value (Dollars only)	Rate	Duty

G. O. No. ....

CERTIFICATE OF LADING FOR TRANSPORTATION IN BOND AND/OR LADING FOR EXPORTATION FOR

.... (Port)

WITH THE EXCEPTIONS NOTED ABOVE, THE WITHIN-DESCRIBED GOODS WERE:

Delivered to the Carrier named above, for delivery to the District Director of Customs at destination sealed with Customs seals Nos. .... or the packages (were) (were not) labeled, or corded and sealed.

.... *(Inspector or warehouse officer)*

.... *(Date)*

Laden on the— .... *(Vessel, vehicle, or aircraft)*

which cleared for— ....

on .... *(Date)*

as verified by export records.

.... *(Inspector)*

.... *(Date)*

I truly declare that the statements contained herein are true and correct to the best of my knowledge and belief.

Entered or withdrawn by ....

....

To the Inspector or Warehouse Officer: The above-described goods shall be disposed of as specified herein.

.... *For the District Director of Customs.*

RECEIVED from the District Director of Customs of above district the merchandise described in this manifest for transportation and delivery into the custody of the customs officers at the port named above, all packages in apparent good order except as noted hereon.

....

.... *Attorney or Agent of Carrier.*

Figure 5.4 Certificate of Origin

Managing the Business 97

Figure 5.5 Consular Invoice

Supplier (name, address, country)	DECLARATION OF ORIGIN— for the export of goods to the REPUBLIC OF SOUTH AFRICA
Consignee (name, address, country)	**NOTE TO IMPORTERS** This declaration, properly completed by the supplier, must be furnished in support of the relative bill of entry where goods qualify for and are entered at the rate of duty lower than the general rate
Particulars of transport	Customs date stamp

1 Item No.	2 Marks and numbers	3 No. and desc. of packages	4 Description of goods	5 Country of origin	6 Gross Mass	7 Invoice No./Ref.

I, (name and capacity)
duly authorised by the supplier of the goods enumerated above hereby declare that—

1. the goods enumerated opposite item(s) _____ in column 1 above have been wholly produced or manufactured in the country stated in column 5 in respect of such goods from raw materials produced in that country;

2. the goods enumerated opposite item(s) _____ in column 1 above have been wholly or partly manufactured from imported materials in the country specified in column 5 in respect of such goods; and

   2.1 the final process of manufacture has taken place in the said country;

   2.2 the cost to the manufacturer of the materials wholly produced or manufactured in the said country plus the cost of labour directly employed in the manufacture of such goods is not less than _____ per cent of the total production cost of such goods;

   2.3 in calculating the production cost of such goods only the cost to the manufacturer of all materials plus manufacturing wages and salaries, direct manufacturing expenses, overhead factory expenses, cost of inside containers and other expenses incidental to manufacturing, used or expended in the manufacture of such goods have been included and profits and administrative, distribution and selling overhead expenses have been excluded.

Place _____ Date _____ Signature of Deponent _____

98 Chapter 5

Figure 5.6 Commercial Invoice

Figure 5.7 Request to Dispose of Commodities or Technical Data Previously Exported

FORM DIB-699P (7-76)
OMB No. 41-R1569

CONFIDENTIAL - Information furnished herewith is deemed confidential and will not be published or disclosed except in accordance with Section 7 of the Export Administration Act of 1969

U.S. DEPARTMENT OF COMMERCE
DOMESTIC AND INTERNATIONAL BUSINESS ADMINISTRATION
BUREAU OF EAST-WEST TRADE
OFFICE OF EXPORT ADMINISTRATION
WASHINGTON, D.C. 20230

CASE NO. (*Leave Blank*)

REQUEST TO DISPOSE OF COMMODITIES OR TECHNICAL DATA PREVIOUSLY EXPORTED

1. DATE OF REQUEST

2(a). APPLICANT'S REF. NO.

2(b). APPLICANT'S TELEPHONE NO.

3. APPLICANT'S NAME

STREET

CITY, STATE, ZIP CODE

4. COMMODITIES OR TECHNICAL DATA PREVIOUSLY EXPORTED UNDER:

VALIDATED LICENSE NO. ______

CASE NO. ______

GENERAL LICENSE (*specify type*) ______

5. NEW ULTIMATE CONSIGNEE

NAME

STREET

CITY AND COUNTRY

6. ORIGINAL ULTIMATE CONSIGNEE

NAME

STREET

CITY AND COUNTRY

7. I (WE) HEREBY REQUEST AUTHORIZATION TO ☐ REEXPORT ☐ SELL

☐ OTHER (*Specify*) ______

THE FOLLOWING: (*If this request is being submitted on behalf of another firm or individual, explain in Item 10 below.*)

8.(a) QUANTITY	(b) DESCRIPTION OF COMMODITY OR TECHNICAL DATA	(c) EXPORT CONTROL COMMODITY NO. AND PROCESSING NO.	(d) DOLLAR VALUE

9. END USE OF COMMODITIES OR TECHNICAL DATA BY NEW ULTIMATE CONSIGNEE (*Describe fully*)

10. ADDITIONAL INFORMATION (*Attach separate sheet if more space is needed*)

11. APPLICANT'S CERTIFICATION - I(We) certify that the above statements are true to the best of my (our) knowledge and belief. If authorization is granted, I(We) will be strictly accountable for its use in accordance with the Export Administration Regulations and all terms and conditions specified on the authorization.

Type or Print ______ (Applicant (*Same as Item 3*))

SIGN HERE IN INK ______ (Signature of person authorized to execute this request)

Type or Print ______ (Name and title of person whose signature appears on line to left)

FOR OFFICIAL USE ONLY

SPECIAL CONDITIONS

ACTION TAKEN	AUTHORITY	RATING	DV	TECH. DATA	
☐ APPROVED ☐ REJECTED		END USE CHECK / RE-EX-PORT	SUPPORT. DOCUMENT	TYPE OF LICENSE	(Licensing officer) (No.) (Date)
DOCUMENTATION					(Review officer) (Date)

NOTE: Submit Form DIB-623P or FC-420 (Application Processing Card) and the first four copies of this request to the Office of Export Administration, Room 1617M, Domestic and International Business Administration, U.S. Department of Commerce, Washington, D.C. 20230 retaining the quintuplicate for your files. This form may be reproduced provided the content, format, size and color of paper and ink are the same.

ORIGINAL
(O E A CASE FILE COPY)

Figure 5.8 Shipper's Export Declaration

Form No.
7525-V
(12-10-73)

Form Approved: O.M.B. No. 41-R0397

U.S. DEPARTMENT OF COMMERCE - SESA, BUREAU OF THE CENSUS - DIBA, BUREAU OF EAST-WEST TRADE

SHIPPER'S EXPORT DECLARATION
OF SHIPMENTS FROM THE UNITED STATES

Export Shipments Are Subject To Inspection By U.S. Customs Service and/or The Office of Export Control

READ CAREFULLY THE INSTRUCTIONS ON BACK TO AVOID DELAY AT SHIPPING POINT

Declarations Should be Typewritten or Prepared in Ink

CONFIDENTIAL For use solely for official purposes authorized by the Secretary of Commerce. Use for unauthorized purposes is not permitted. (Title 15, Sec. 30.91(a) C.F.R.; Sec. 7(c) Export Administration Act of 1969, as amended, P.L. 91-184).

Authentication (*When required*)

Do Not Use This Area	District	Port	Country	(For customs use only)

FILE NO. (For Customs use only.)

1. FROM (*U.S. Port of Export*)

2. METHOD OF TRANSPORTATION (*check one*):
☐ Vessel (INCL. FERRY) ☐ Air ☐ Other (*Specify*)

2a. EXPORTING CARRIER (*If vessel, give name of ship, flag and pier number. If air, give name of airline.*)

3. EXPORTER (*Principal or seller — licensee*) ADDRESS (*Number, street, place, state*)

4. AGENT OF EXPORTER (*Forwarding agent*) ADDRESS (*Number, street, place, state*)

5. ULTIMATE CONSIGNEE ADDRESS (*Place, country*)

6. INTERMEDIATE CONSIGNEE ADDRESS (*Place, country*)

7. FOREIGN PORT OF UNLOADING (*For vessel and air shipments only*)

8. PLACE AND COUNTRY OF ULTIMATE DESTINATION (*Not place of transshipment*)

(9) MARKS AND NOS	(10) NUMBER AND KIND OF PACKAGES, DESCRIPTION OF COMMODITIES, EXPORT LICENSE NUMBER, EXPIRATION DATE (OR GENERAL LICENSE SYMBOL) (Describe commodities in sufficient detail to permit verification of the Schedule B commodity numbers assigned. Do not use general terms.)	(11) SHIPPING (*Gross*) WEIGHT IN POUNDS a (required for vessel and air shipments only)	(12) SPECIFY "D" OR "F" b	(13) SCHEDULE B COMMODITY NO (*Include Commodity Control List italicized digit when required*)	(14) NET QUANTITY IN SCHEDULE B UNITS (*State unit*)	(15) VALUE AT U.S. PORT OF EXPORT (Selling price or cost if not sold, including inland freight, insurance and other charges to U.S. port of export) (*Nearest whole dollar omit cents figures*)

These commodities licensed by U.S. for ultimate destination .... Diversion contrary to U.S. law prohibited.
VALIDATED LICENSE NO. OR GENERAL LICENSE SYMBOL

16. BILL OF LADING OR AIR WAYBILL NUMBER

17. DATE OF EXPORTATION (*Not required for shipments by vessel*)

18. THE UNDERSIGNED HEREBY AUTHORIZES ______________________ (Name and address—Number, street, place, State)
TO ACT AS FORWARDING AGENT FOR EXPORT CONTROL AND CUSTOMS PURPOSES.

EXPORTER ______________________ BY (DULY AUTHORIZED OFFICER OR EMPLOYEE) ______________________

► 19. I CERTIFY THAT ALL STATEMENTS MADE AND ALL INFORMATION CONTAINED IN THIS EXPORT DECLARATION ARE TRUE AND CORRECT. I AM AWARE OF THE PENALTIES PROVIDED FOR FALSE REPRESENTATION. (*See Paragraphs I (c), (e), on reverse side.*)

Signature ______________________ (Duly authorized officer or employee of exporter or named forwarding agent) For ______________________ (Name of corporation or firm, and capacity of signer; e.g., secretary, export manager, etc.)

Address ______________________

► Declaration should be made by duly authorized officer or employee of exporter or of forwarding agent named by exporter.
a. If shipping weight is not available for each Schedule B item listed in column (13) included in one or more packages, insert the approximate gross weight for each Schedule B item. The total of these estimated weights should equal the actual weight of the entire package or packages.
b. Designate foreign merchandise (reexports) with an "F" and exports of domestic merchandise produced in the United States or changed in condition in the United States with a "D". (*See instructions on reverse side.*)

Do Not Use This Area

Figure 5.9 Request for Notice of Amendment Action

FORM DIB-685P (Formerly IA-763)
(Revised 4-74)

U.S. DEPARTMENT OF COMMERCE
DOMESTIC AND INTERNATIONAL BUSINESS ADMINISTRATION
BUREAU OF EAST-WEST TRADE
OFFICE OF EXPORT ADMINISTRATION

FORM APPROVED. OMB NO. 41-R1186

THIS SPACE FOR OFFICIAL USE ONLY

REQUEST FOR AND NOTICE OF AMENDMENT ACTION

1. CASE NO.

3. LICENSE NO.

2. APPLICANT'S REFERENCE NO.

4. EXPIRATION DATE OF LICENSE

5. RETURN COPY OF AMENDMENT NOTICE TO

6. NAME OF LICENSEE

7. COUNTRY OF ULTIMATE DESTINATION

8. DATES OF PREVIOUS EXTENSIONS (If any)

9. COMMODITY DESCRIPTION

10. EXPORT CONTROL COMMODITY NO.

11. PROCESSING NUMBER

12. FACTS NECESSITATING AMENDMENT

VALIDATION

☐ APPROVED ☐ REJECTED

(Signature of licensing officer) (Date)

REASON FOR REJECTION

13. AMEND LICENSE TO READ AS FOLLOWS:

14. HAS THIS REQUEST BEEN PREVIOUSLY REJECTED OR IS IT PENDING IN ANY COMMERCE DEPARTMENT OFFICE? IF YES, EXPLAIN ON SEPARATE SHEET. ☐ YES ☐ NO

15. SIGNATURE

(Licensee)

BY (Authorized agent) (Title) (Date)

Chapter 5

Figure 5.10 Request for Status

Managing the Business   103

Figure 5.11 Export License

FORM DIB-628 (REV. 1-75)	Not approved unless the official validation stamp appears hereon.
EXPORT LICENSE	LICENSE NUMBER
U.S. DEPARTMENT OF COMMERCE	VALIDATION
DOMESTIC AND INTERNATIONAL BUSINESS ADMINISTRATION	
BUREAU OF EAST-WEST TRADE	
OFFICE OF EXPORT ADMINISTRATION	

License is hereby granted to the licensee named herein, upon the terms and provisions stated herein, to export from the United States the articles, materials, technical data, or supplies herein described. This license is granted in reliance on representations heretofore made by the licensee to obtain it and is expressly subject to all export control laws, regulations, rules, and orders. It is not transferable without written permission from the Office of Export Administration.

1. LICENSEE	2. PURCHASER
3. ULTIMATE CONSIGNEE IN FOREIGN COUNTRY	4. INTERMEDIATE CONSIGNEE
5. COUNTRY OF ULTIMATE DESTINATION	6. APPLICANT'S REFERENCE NO.

QUANTITY	DESCRIPTION OF COMMODITIES	EXPORT CONTROL COMMODITY NUMBER AND PROCESSING NUMBER	UNIT PRICE	TOTAL PRICE
			TOTAL	

NOTE:
- An Export License must be returned immediately to the Office of Export Administration, Room 1617M, Domestic and International Business Administration, U. S. Department of Commerce, Washington, D.C. 20230, (a) when it has been fully used, (b) when it has expired, or (c) when it has been determined that it will not be used or will no longer be used.
- Each shipment made against this license shall be entered on the reverse and licensee must sign prior to returning it.
- A <u>Destination Control Statement</u> is required to be shown on all bills of lading, air waybills, and commercial invoices. (See Export Administration Regulations § 386.6.)

Figure 5.12 Application for Export License

CERTIFICATE OF ORIGIN

SHIPPER/EXPORTER	DOCUMENT NO.
	EXPORT REFERENCES
CONSIGNEE	FORWARDING AGENT - REFERENCES
	POINT AND COUNTRY OF ORIGIN
NOTIFY PARTY	DOMESTIC ROUTING/EXPORT INSTRUCTIONS
PIER OR AIRPORT	
EXPORTING CARRIER (Vessel/Airline) / PORT OF LOADING	ONWARD INLAND ROUTING
AIR/SEA PORT OF DISCHARGE / FOR TRANSSHIPMENT TO	

PARTICULARS FURNISHED BY SHIPPER

MARKS AND NUMBERS	NO. OF PKGS.	DESCRIPTION OF PACKAGES AND GOODS	GROSS WEIGHT	MEASUREMENT

The undersigned _____ (Owner or Agent), does hereby declare for the above named shipper, the goods as described above were shipped on the above date and consigned as indicated and are products of the United States of America.

Dated at _____ on the _____ day of _____ 19____
Sworn to before me this _____ day of _____ 19____

SIGNATURE OF OWNER OR AGENT

The _____, a recognized Chamber of Commerce under the laws of the State of _____, has examined the manufacturer's invoice or shipper's affidavit concerning the origin of the merchandise, and, according to the best of its knowledge and belief, finds that the products named orginated in the United States of North America.

Secretary _____

CHAPTER 6

AFTER THE SALE

Generating sales is important, but it isn't all there is to operating a business overseas. So that we don't go too far afield, let's limit our postsales considerations to two issues:

- Getting paid for what you've sold; and

- Being able to service your product (assuming you sell goods, rather than services).

Getting Paid

Everyone who has been in business for any length of time has had a collection problem of one type or another. Imagine how much more difficult that problem must be when the other party is 5,000 miles away, uses different business procedures and business forms, operates under a different set of laws, uses a different currency, and speaks a different language.

The most common methods of payment are:

- Cash in advance
- Letter of credit
- Documentary draft
- Open account
- Consignment

Overseas, as here, the deciding factor in setting the terms of payment is the amount of trust one has in another's ability to pay. If a great deal of trust exists, either because of the other party's reputation or because of previous dealings that have proved satisfactory, then sales often are made on an open account. If this level of trust does not exist, then the buyer frequently is asked for cash in advance. In between, there are several other options.

Cash in Advance

For the exporter, this is easily the most preferable type of payment. There are no billing and collection delays. There is no collection risk. And the money is immediately in hand for other use.

For the buyer, on the other hand, this is possibly the worst form of payment. The money is expended before the merchandise is received, thus forcing the buyer to demonstrate all of the trust. If the merchandise is defective, the wrong merchandise delivered, the delivery delayed, or any other problem arises, the buyer must wage the battle for restitution from a greatly weakened position.

More equitable terms of payment generally are negotiated, particularly when sizeable sums are involved.

Letters of Credit

When a firm is new to the export market or is entering a particular world market for the first time, the use of a letter of credit generally is preferred.

In this situation, some third party—usually a bank—acts as a intermediary to assure that the other two parties perform as agreed. Documents, such as shipping and insurance forms, are required to prove that the conditions of the sale have been met.

For speedier and easier handling, two intermediaries are commonly involved—one in the exporter's country and one in the buyer's. Often, these are two branches of the same bank or two banks that frequently work together.

When a letter of intent is involved, the exporter presents documents to the designated U.S. bank to prove that the goods have been shipped according to the terms specified in the shipping order. The bank then pays the exporter according to the pre-arranged terms, either on the spot or at a later date, usually 30, 60, or 90 days later.

The letter of credit is a document issued by a bank, at the request of the buyer, in favor of the exporter. Essentially, it is the bank's promise to pay a specific sum of money upon receipt of certain documents and within a specified time. The documents ensure that the terms of the sale, as stated in the letter of credit, have been met. These terms may include quantity of merchandise, method of shipment, shipping date, insurance coverage, and so on.

A letter of credit may be *revocable* or *irrevocable.* Since a revocable letter of credit may be altered or revoked without the exporter's permission or knowledge, an irrevocable letter of credit is preferred. If the letter of credit is irrevocable, the bank must make payment, even if the buyer defaults.

In addition, the exporter may have the letter of credit *confirmed* by a U.S. bank. If so, then the U.S. bank is required to pay the exporter, even if the buyer's foreign bank defaults. This can be of particular value if the foreign bank does not have a sound record, or if the country involved is not politically or economically sound.

Generally, the U.S. bank will pay the exporter promptly when there is an unconfirmed letter of credit, but occasionally one may refuse to do so until it has received payment from the foreign bank. Even if the exporter has been paid, however, he is still liable to the U.S. bank if the foreign bank defaults on the unconfirmed letter of credit.

The following will illustrate what typically transpires when payment is assured by an irrevocable letter of credit, confirmed by a U.S. bank:

> The exporter and his customer agree on the terms of a sale, and the buyer arranges for his bank to open an irrevocable letter of credit, including all instructions to the exporter regarding the shipment. The buyer's bank sends this letter to a U.S. bank and requests confirmation.
>
> The U.S. bank prepares a letter of confirmation and forwards it and the irrevocable letter of credit to the exporter.
>
> The exporter reviews the conditions specified in the letter of credit. The exporter will consult with his shipping agent to be sure that the shipping date(s) can be met. If there are any conditions that the exporter feels he cannot satisfy, he should alert the buyer immediately. All conditions must be met precisely, or the letter of credit may be invalid. If the exporter cannot meet any of the terms, as stated, or even if he finds something that has been misspelled, he should ask the buyer for an amendment to the letter of credit.
>
> If everything proceeds satisfactorily, the exporter will arrange for his freight forwarder to deliver the merchandise to the appropriate port or air terminal. After the merchandise has been loaded, the forwarder will complete the necessary documents.
>
> Either the exporter or the freight forwarder will present the U.S. bank with documents proving that the terms of the order have been met. If the bank finds that the documentation is in order, it will pay the exporter.
>
> The U.S. bank will then air-mail the documents to the foreign bank, which will review them and then forward them to the buyer. In that manner, the buyer—or his agent—receives the documents that are needed to claim the merchandise.

Both the exporter's bank and the buyer's bank will charge a fee for their services in handling the letter of credit. This fee generally ranges from one-quarter of one percent to a full one percent of the amount of payment, and is usually charged to the buyer's account—although this must be specifically stated in all quotations. If the buyer refuses to accept the added charges, the exporter may wish to absorb them rather than lose the sale, especially if the buyer is a new customer or if the foreign bank or foreign government are of questionable security.

Banks will not pay any more than what is specified in the letter of credit, even when the exporter can document that higher shipping, insurance or other charges have been incurred. This should be remembered when preparing quotations.

Be meticulous when dealing with letters of credit. Among the most common mistakes are:

- Late shipment;
- Documents that are not properly signed or dated;
- Late presentation of documents; and
- Presenting "unclean" documents, i.e. ones that reflect irregularities or damage at the time the shipment is made.

Documentary Drafts

A documentary draft, sometimes called a *bill of exchange*, is similar to a letter of credit. Once again, a third-party intermediary is involved. In this case, however, the buyer pays a bank in his own country for the merchandise, then receives the documents required to acquire the goods. Drafts used in this sort of transaction can be *sight* drafts, *time* drafts or *date* drafts.

A *sight* draft allows the exporter to retain title to his shipment until it reaches its destination and is paid for. The bill of lading or airway bill is endorsed by the shipper and sent to the buyer's bank (or other intermediary) along with a sight draft, invoices and other documents (packing lists, consular invoices, insurance certificates, etc.) required either by the buyer or the buyer's country. The buyer's bank then notifies the buyer and, as soon as the amount of the draft is paid, turns over the bill of lading that enables the buyer to accept the shipment.

There is some risk in using a sight draft as a means of payment. Between the time the shipment is made and the time the draft is presented for payment, the buyer can undergo some change in his ability or willingness to pay for the merchandise, or the policies of the importing country may change.

If the buyer does not pay for and claim the shipment, the exporter is responsible for it and must either have it returned or try to sell it elsewhere.

By accepting a *time* draft or a *date* draft, the exporter is extending a type of credit to his customer. Both are similar documents and call for payment within a certain time (30, 60, 90 days, or longer) or by a certain date (such as June 11) after the buyer has received the merchandise and accepted the draft. Once the buyer writes "accepted" on the draft and signs it, he is obligated to make payment within the specified time.

Once a time draft or a date draft has been signed off, the draft becomes a *trade acceptance* and can be either held by the exporter until due or sold to a bank for immediate payment. If the draft is sold to a bank, the bank will "discount" the amount it pays to the exporter in exchange for advancing the funds before they are actually due.

If a sight draft or a time draft is used, the buyer can gain some valuable time by delaying acceptance of the draft, thereby delaying the time he must make payment for the goods. A date draft will prevent this abuse.

Banks generally charge a smaller fee for handling drafts than for handling letters of credit.

Open Accounts

Open accounts can be risky for the exporter unless the customer is well known to him or unless a thorough credit check has been conducted.

Furthermore, the exporter's money is tied up in the shipment until payment has been received and, in most cases, that will not be until after the shipment has been received. Even then, many companies are not particularly punctual in dealing with their Accounts Payable.

Consignments

Sales on consignment work the same abroad as they do in the U.S.: merchandise is shipped to a distributor, who attempts to sell it for the exporter. The exporter holds title to the merchandise until it is sold, at which time payment is sent to the exporter, less the distributor's sales commission. Obviously, the exporter has little control over the situation and may have to wait a considerable period of time before he is paid.

When this type of arrangement is used, exporters would be wise to conduct an extensive credit check of the distributor in question, investigate some type of political risk insurance and establish who will be responsible for risk insurance on the merchandise while it is in the distributor's possession.

Countertrade And Barter

In many developing and Eastern European countries, the governments have high foreign trade deficits, large international debts and small foreign currencies holdings. This limits the amount of foreign exchange that importers have available to pay for merchandise. If an exporter wishes to do business in those countries, some type of countertrade may be necessary.

Countertrade is more complex than barter, which is simply a direct exchange of goods or services between two parties. Countertrade involves the exchange of some currency as well. For example, a countertrade contract may specify that the exporter will be paid in currency *if* he agrees to find markets for certain products from the buyer's country. Variations of countertrade include compensation trade, buy-back, counterpurchase, and offset.

Since countertrade transactions are very complex and hard to arrange, a large corporation, international bank, or trading company usually sets them up. Small- or medium-sized exporters can engage in countertrade, however, by working through one of the larger intermediaries. Some trading houses also offer countertrade services.

On the negative side, an exporter who handles a countertrade transaction alone must sell not only his own products but also the merchandise that he acquires as a result of the transaction. Products involved in countertrade often have to be discounted 20 percent or more. Also, very high fees are usually charged in countertrade transactions. Be aware, too, that nearly everything involved in one of these transactions is doubled *except the profit*—*two* shipments, *two* customs clearances and *two* times as many opportunities for something to go wrong.

U.S. exporters can obtain advice and assistance regarding countertrade from the Office of Trade Finance, International Trade Administration, U.S. Department of Commerce, Washington, D.C.; (202)377-3277. This assistance involves the collection of needed information; the identification of options, risks and problems; and aid in locating sources of help in the private sector.

Foreign Exchange

The best way to be sure that you are getting the kind of deal you thought you had arranged is to quote prices and demand payment *in U.S. dollars*. If you don't, variations in the rates at which world currencies are exchanged can make a sweet deal turn sour almost overnight. For example:

> It is April 1989 and you are in Haiti to quote an order. The Haitian gourde is valued at $.20 so you quote a price of 500,000 gourdes for the merchandise, expecting to receive $100,000 in payment.
>
> But, before you can get home and put the shipment together, the value of the gourde slips *one penny*. With the gourde valued at $.19 instead of $.20, the buyer's payment of 500,000 gourdes adds up to $95,000, not $100,000. You

have lost $5,000 by quoting your merchandise in gourdes rather than in dollars!

True, the rates of exchange fluctuate in both directions, and you might have received *more* than $100,000 on the Haitian deal if the value of the gourde had risen instead of decreased. But speculation on the value of world currencies is the business of bankers, not businesspeople. If you want to avoid surprises, deal with factors that you know and understand.

If a customer asks to make payment in a currency other than U.S. dollars, consult an international banker. Such bankers not only can give you advice but, when called upon, often agree to pay a fixed price for the foreign currency, regardless of the exchange rate at the time payment is received. For assuming this additional risk, the bank will charge you a fee and, if you decide to enter into a contract on that basis, the bank's fee should be added into your price quotation.

If Things Go Wrong . . .

It is easier to avoid a problem than it is to correct one.

You can buy insurance to protect yourself against commercial credit risks, but before a claim will be honored, you must have exhausted every reasonable means of obtaining payment. Even then, you may have to wait a long time before the insurance payment actually is received.

Arbitration may work, and it is faster and less expensive than taking legal action. Most arbitration abroad is handled through the International Chamber of Commerce, which has a Vice President for Arbitration in New York—(212)354-4480. The American Arbitration Association, also located in New York, offers services abroad—(212)484-4000.

If a U.S. exporter is involved in a dispute arising from a specific overseas transaction and the other party simply refuses to discuss the matter, a complaint may be processed through one of the U.S. Department of Commerce District Offices. Before getting their help, however, the exporter must have made every effort to settle the dispute and the claim must be in excess of $1,000; the Commerce Department will then intercede in an attempt to get both parties talking again. If the issue ultimately goes to court, however, the Commerce Department usually will withdraw from the matter.

Servicing Your Product

A good relationship with your overseas distributor is extremely valuable, of course, but any company's long-term success as an exporter will depend on how well it establishes a favorable relationship with the end-user of its product(s). Customer satisfaction, of course, entails the delivery of a quality product at a reasonable price. But also, customers will expect the product to perform well for a reasonable period of time (determined by historical standards associated with products of a similar type) and, barring that, to be able to repair the product conveniently, quickly, and affordably.

How to set up an effective servicing program overseas?

Six approaches are available:

- Ignore the matter of service entirely.
- Find a local organization to service your product(s).
- Set up your own overseas service facility.
- Train your distributor's personnel to service and maintain your product(s).
- Set up a service organization in cooperation with other companies that have similar servicing needs.
- Have the customer send the product(s) to the U.S. for servicing.

Each of these options has certain advantages and disadvantages.

The first option is best suited for inexpensive and/or disposable products. There is no need to repair a disposable product. If the customer would prefer to buy a new widget than repair the old one, then setting up a service facility for widgets doesn't make much sense.

After the Sale 115

The second and third options are the most expensive. This can make it difficult for an exporter to be cost-competitive *unless* his product is rather expensive *or* it is highly proprietary.

The second option—use of a local company to service the product—is not only expensive, but it presents several other disadvantages:

- Preparing the local company through training, providing it with a suitable inventory of spare parts, and supplying it with other necessary diagnostic or repair equipment can be difficult and costly.

- The exporter may not have a great deal of control over the service company, its personnel, or its business practices.

- The local company may give a low priority to the exporter's work.

- Responsibility cannot be delegated, so the customer probably will blame a poor service experience on the manufacturer, rather than the local service company.

The third option—setting up an overseas service facility—can be cost-prohibitive for a small company or a company just beginning to enter the market. There are many long-term advantages to this approach, of course.

The fourth option may be the best compromise *if* the distributor is agreeable and capable of doing the job. On the other hand, such an arrangement creates a stronger tie to the distributor than may be preferable.

The fifth option gives the exporter a local presence and a larger measure of control, yet it is less expensive than most other options because of the shared costs. This approach may take longer to set up, however.

And finally, the sixth option will be impractical if your product(s) are large and/or unusually heavy. You can hardly expect a customer to air express a refrigerator to the U.S. for repairs.

Whatever method of servicing an exporter chooses, it is certain that service is one of his most important marketing tools. It will be well received by his domestic and foreign business associates, including distributors, bankers, and customers. It is also a symbol of his commitment to the market.

CHAPTER 7

OTHER AVENUES TO PURSUE

Involvement in international trade is not limited to a make-it-here, sell-it-there scenario. Some other possibilities include:

- Setting up an overseas manufacturing facility;
- Setting up a wholly-owned foreign sales facility;
- Licensing your technology to a foreign company that can make and market the product abroad;
- Forming a joint venture with a foreign company through which you both actively participate;
- Franchising your company and selling franchises overseas;
- Countertrade; and
- Re-export.

Some of these need no elaboration. An overseas manufacturing facility, for example, might produce labor savings, put the company closer to the source of raw materials, enable the company to buy raw materials at less cost, and (almost certainly) reduce shipping costs. An overseas sales facility might provide greater control, reduce personnel training expenses, reduce employee turnover, assure greater concentration on the marketing of your product and save on sales expenses.

Joint ventures, licensing, franchising and countertrade warrant some additional discussion.

Joint Ventures

Forming a joint venture is like forming a partnership with another company for the purpose of doing business together. You may each have equal shares or unequal shares (in some countries, the local firm must own a 51 percent interest).

A joint venture may be an advantage over a wholly-owned facility. In some countries, there are laws requiring a purchase from local sources, if possible. In other countries, the law mandates that the local firm gets the business *unless a foreign bid is notably lower*.

In addition, the overseas partner may have a great deal to contribute to the enterprise—special technology, critical patents, excellent customer contacts, a large marketing capability, money, and so on.

Joint ventures can be a very useful way to enter the international market. It brings new capital to the business and it helps to spread the high costs and risks of expansion.

One's foreign business partners also may have a number of other valuable contributions to make:

- Knowledge of the local customs and tastes
- An established distribution network
- An established local reputation
- Solid customer, business, banking, and/or political contacts
- On-site personnel to help overcome language problems and day-to-day supervisory needs

On the other hand, one may have to deal not only with a prospective business partner, but with government agencies, when setting up a joint venture. In situations where government regulations call for the resident partner to have a controlling interest in the business, the U.S. partner will lose some of its control, which can lead to increased costs, reduced profits, inferior quality, and exposure to certain product liability or environmental difficulties.

If the licensing of technology is involved in a joint venture, antitrust issues may come under investigation as well. It would be wise to obtain an *export trade certificate of review* from the U.S. Department of Commerce and/or a *Business Review Letter* from the U.S. Department of Justice if there is any possibility that such difficulties could arise.

In virtually every case, it is wise to obtain legal counsel within the foreign country in which you intend to do business, in addition to your U.S. counsel. The foreign counsel can help your company obtain government approvals and can advise you on such matters as trademarks, copyrights, patents, and so on.

A useful publication to explore is the *Antitrust Guide Concerning Research Joint Ventures*, available from the Justice Department.

Good legal counsel is always advisable.

Licensing

Licensing allows an American company to enter foreign markets quickly, and it may help avoid certain tariff or non-tariff barriers that host countries have imposed. It can be particularly good for a small company or for one with very little international experience.

The use of the technology, for instance, generally is paid for in the form of royalties, which may come in a lump sum, as "running" royalties (that is, royalties that are paid according to the amount of volume involved) or as some combination of the two. Some governments impose limitations on the royalties that are allowed.

This is not to say that licensing does not have its share of problems. In some Third World countries, for example, inadequate regulation of such agreements may lead to the unauthorized use of your company's technology by your overseas partner or by others. One way to quickly assess a potential partner's viability is to see if his country has a tax treaty or a bilateral investment treaty with the

U.S. If it does, your risks will be lessened but still not totally eliminated.

If the technology involved is highly advanced, you may be required to obtain an export license from the U.S. Department of Commerce.

Certain questions regarding antitrust may be raised. Be sure to familiarize yourself with the *Antitrust Guide for International Operations*, available from the Justice Department and (if the business involves the new Common Market) *Commission Regulation [EEC] No. 22349/84* on the *Application of Article 85(3) of the Treaty [of Rome] to Certain Categories of Patent Licensing Agreements*, which became effective in 1985.

When a company engages in licensing, it is well advised to impose specific territorial restrictions on the agreement. Otherwise, it may finditself competing with itself for market segments that were totally unexpected.

Licensing is simply a contractual agreement to permit another party to use your patents, service marks, trademarks, copyrights, and other knowledge or assets. For that privilege, the licensee pays a royalty, which may come in a lump sum or involve on-going payments, generally determined on the basis of a certain fee for each unit produced or sold. Sometimes, the transaction will involve both forms of payment.

Licensing permits you to enter a new market quickly. It involves less initial investment than setting up a wholly-owned manufacturing plant. It also can short-circuit other financial and legal risks, including possible tariff and non-tariff barriers that could be encountered if the product were made in the U.S. and then exported.

Franchising

Franchising is a form of licensing, commonly applied to the service industries.

EC92 has issued a "block exemption" to encourage franchising in Europe, where it has become immensely popular. And since the first step in establishing a franchise is to register your trademark, the ability to do so once, rather than having to do so in each country, is a tremendous advantage.

Be aware that local preferences may call for some modifications in the way business is conducted. A good product, marketed well, will succeed anywhere, but merchandising "gimmicks" that work here may not work there. Names that have local or regional appeal here may have no appeal elsewhere. Direct mail advertising, popular here, is more expensive and less common in other parts of the world.

American franchises are popular overseas for a number of reasons:

- The dollar is down, making a franchise less expensive to foreign buyers.

- The U.S. is the acknowledged world-leader in mass-marketing.

Another consideration: franchising often presents "fail-safe" guides to effective management—the very thing that East Europeans for instance, need the most.

Franchising is particularly appealing because it affords almost limitless variety.

See a void in the market? There's sure to be a franchise available that will fill it. Have a limited amount of money to invest? There's certainly something available within your price range. Know a little something about carpentry, or cooking, or barbering? Shop around and you will find some franchise that suits your interests.

As a result, franchises are very popular in most overseas markets. They were, in fact, one of the first classes of business to be cleared by those who have the responsibility to set the standards for EC92, and they are particularly popular in Eastern Europe.

How do you explain the popularity of franchises in Eastern Europe? It's quite simple, really. The companies within the Eastern Bloc have had virtually no experience in managing a business according to the concepts of free enterprise. Since virtually all franchises come with a very detailed operational and management package already in place, a franchise helps to offset a business person's lack of expertise and experience.

So much for the benefits of *buying* a franchise for an overseas market. The opposite side of the coin, of course, involves packaging and *selling* a franchise abroad.

Many franchise firms have had considerable success in the overseas markets for the reasons cited above. A new firm must be sure that its market niche is not already overcrowded. Assuming that it is not, it needs to be checked to be sure that it conforms to the legal requirements in *each of the countries in which it hopes to do business.* That is one of the benefits of EC92: Instead of having to accommodate the laws of a number of different nations, it is possible now to accommodate only one set of requirements in order to do business on the entire continent.

Naturally those who are considering a franchise will have a few questions other than those related to cost and area of activity. Specifically, they will be anxious to know:

- Will a source of business aid be available locally, or will it be necessary to wait until we get assistance from the franchise headquarters in the U.S.?

- Does the franchise enjoy a good local reputation or must we establish a position of our own?

- If competitive businesses exist, how does our franchise compare as to quality, cost, reputation, management, marketing, profitability, and so on?

- How long has the franchise company been doing business in this country?

- How many franchises does the company have in this country?

- What is the company's track record in this country?

The answers to these questions can be very important.

When a company needs help, it rarely can afford the time to wait until the home office gets around to answering a letter or until it has an opportunity to fly someone in. If a company seriously considers offering franchises in a foreign market, it would be well advised to set up an office in that market to service its local clients promptly.

A franchise that already enjoys a strong, favorable reputation in the market will help a business establish itself and attain profitability more quickly. If it's an unknown, then the buyer should not be expected to pay as much for the franchise as he would if he were buying a franchise in the U.S. where the company might be better known.

It is particularly important for a franchise well-removed from the parent to investigate the parent's financial health and stability. If the parent goes down the tubes, the franchise is left high and dry with little recourse.

The term "countertrade" is a catchall for transactions that are not paid for solely in currency. The transaction may call for barter, compensation trade, buy-back, counterpurchase, or offset.

Such transactions are most common with Third World countries in which money is scarce. Such countries may even have a law that requires such transactions.

Small exporters should avoid this type of transaction unless they are absolutely certain that they will be able to dispose of the merchandise—wine, grain, or what-have-you—that they receive in payment. They also must be sure that the merchandise will be admitted to the U.S., that it has been valued fairly, and so on. There are "barter houses" and countertrade departments in some large banks that will help you to dispose of such goods for a fee.

Another consideration: if you deal through countertrade, there will be *two* shipments to handle. That will mean two sets of documentation, two customs clearances—two of everything.

This is not to discourage such trading in general. Although it may be more trouble than the small business cares to handle, larger companies may be able to gain from it. PepsiCo, for example, has been getting some of its profits out of the USSR in the form of vodka and ocean vessels.

Countertrade should result in a fair and profitable transaction, and should not be seen or used as a means of economic blackmail.

Such transactions can be very complex. Help is available from the Office of Trade Finance, U.S. Department of Commerce; (202)377-3277.

CHAPTER 8

HELP FROM YOUR HOME STATE

Fully aware of the fact that exports create economic growth, jobs, and tax revenues, state governments are paying more attention to the needs and interests of businesses seeking to compete in international markets.

In 1987, the export of goods from the U.S. accounted for 5.5 million American jobs. In the manufacturing sector of the economy, one job in every six was due to export. Exports generate 14 percent of the U.S.'s total production. For every billion dollars worth of export, 40,000 U.S. jobs are created.

Spearheading the state-level effort to stimulate increased export has been the U.S. Department of Commerce. It supervises the International Trade Administration—the organization that deals primarily with export. At the state level, your point of contact is the

District Office of the U.S. and Foreign Commercial Service (US&FCS), which provides businesses with information on:

- Trade and investment opportunities overseas;
- Foreign markets for American products and services;
- Organizations that will help you locate and evaluate foreign buyers and representatives;
- Financial aid;
- The U.S. Export-Import Bank;
- Tax benefits;
- International trade shows;
- Export documentation requirements;
- Economic statistics on overseas countries;
- U.S. export licensing requirements; and
- Foreign import requirements.

These district offices also can help you with market research, aid in promoting your product abroad, locating overseas agents or distributors, introductions to foreign buyers, and evaluating customers. They often conduct trade missions abroad, hold export seminars and conferences, and coordinate participation in major international trade fairs.

Operating through the US&FCS District Offices are 51 District Export Councils—groups of experienced volunteers who can advise you on a broad range of matters related to export.

Also actively engaged at the state level is the Small Business Administration, which has field offices throughout the U.S. These offices provide counseling, conduct training programs, operate loan guarantee and direct loan programs, and provide free legal counseling through the International Law Council of the Federal Bar Association. They also supervise the Small Business Institute, through which advanced business students from more than 450 colleges and universities provide small businesses with in-depth, long-term counseling.

State governments also have become involved, along with local chambers of commerce (which often conduct export seminars, workshops, and roundtables; provide certificates of origin [required in export]; set up overseas trade missions; make promotional mailings overseas; organize U.S. pavilions at foreign trade shows; contact foreign companies and distributors; help with transportation routings and the consolidation of shipments; host visiting trade missions; and conduct trade shows at home).

Given such free access to virtually any type of assistance, American businesses have responded enthusiastically.

Following is a partial listing of these agencies in your home state which can give you information, advice, contacts, and many other useful and valuable services. Be sure to ask them for information on other state departments if they can not help you.

Alabama

Birmingham Area Chamber of Commerce, 1914 6th Ave. North, Birmingham 35203, (205)323-5461

U.S. Department of Commerce, US&FCS District Office, Berry Building, 3rd Floor, 2015 2nd Ave. North, Birmingham 35203, (205)254-1331; fax (205)731-0076

U.S. Small Business Administration, 908 S. 20th St., Suite 202, Birmingham 35205, (205)254-1344

Alabama International Trade Center, University of Alabama, Box 870396, Tuscaloosa 35487-0396, (205)348-7621; fax (205)348-6974

Alaska

Alaska Center for International Business, University of Alaska, 4201 Tudor Centre Dr., Suite 120, Anchorage 99508, (907)561-2322; fax (907)561-1541

Anchorage Chamber of Commerce, 415 F St., Anchorage 99501, (907)272-2401

Governor's Office of International Trade, 3601 C. St., Suite 798, Anchorage 99503, (907)561-5585; fax (907)561-4577.

U.S. Department of Commerce, US&FCS District Office, 222 W. 7th Ave., #32, Anchorage 99513, (907)271-5041; fax (907)271-5173

Alaska Department of Commerce & Economic Development, Pouch D, Juneau 99811, (907)465-3580

Alaska State Chamber of Commerce, 310 Second St., Juneau 99801, (907)586-2323

Arizona

Arizona Chamber of Commerce, 1366 E. Thomas St., Phoenix 85014, (602)248-9172

Arizona Department of Commerce, International Trade Division, 3800 N. Central Ave., Suite 1500, Phoenix 85012, (602)280-1371; fax (602)280-1305

Arizona District Export Council, 3412 Federal Building, 230 N. First Ave., Phoenix 85025, (602)261-3285

U.S. Department of Commerce, International Trade Administration, Federal Building & U.S. Courthouse, 230 N. First Ave., Room 3412, Phoenix 85025, (602)261-3285

U.S. Department of Commerce, US&FCS District Office, Federal Building & U.S. Courthouse, 230 N. First Ave., Room 3412, Phoenix 85025, (602)254-3285; fax (602)379-4324

Arkansas

U.S. Department of Commerce, US&FCS District Office, 320 W. Capitol Ave., Room 811, Little Rock 72201-3518, (501)378-5794; fax (501)378-7380

University of Arkansas at Little Rock, International Trade Center, 33rd & University, Little Rock 72204, (501)371-2992

Help From Your Home State   129

California

Economic Development Corporation of Los Angeles County, 1052 W. 6th St., Suite 510, Los Angeles 90017, (213)482-5222

Foreign Trade Association of Southern California, 350 S. Figueroa Ave., #226, Los Angeles 90071, (213)627-0634

Los Angeles International Trade Development Corp., 555 Flower St., #2014, Los Angeles 90071, (213)622-4832

U.S. Department of Commerce, US&FCS District Office, 11000 Wilshire Blvd., Suite 9200, Los Angeles 90024, (213)574-7104; fax (213)575-7220

Northern California District Export Council, 450 Golden Gate Ave., Box 36013, San Francisco 94102, (415)556-5868

San Francisco Chamber of Commerce, 465 California St., San Francisco 94104, (415)392-4511, Ext. 33

San Francisco International Trade Council, P.O. Box 6052, San Francisco 94101, (415)332-9100

U.S. Department of Commerce, US&FCS District Office, Federal Building, Room 15205, 450 Golden Gate Ave., Box 36013, San Francisco 94102, (415)556-5860; fax (415)556-2121

Colorado

International Trade Assn. of Colorado, P.O. Box 18398, Denver 80218, (303)831-1332

U.S. Department of Commerce, US&FCS District Office, 1625 Broadway Ave., Suite 680, Denver 80202, (303)844-3246; fax (303)844-5651

Connecticut

Connecticut Department of Commerce, International Div., 210 Washington St., Hartford 06106, (203)566-5426

Connecticut International Trade Assn., c/o Suisman & Blumenthal, P.O. Box 119, Hartford 06141

U.S. Department of Commerce, US&FCS District Office, Federal Office Building, Room 610-B, 450 Main St., Hartford 06103, (203)240-3530; fax (203)240-3473

Delaware

Delaware Development Office, World Trade Section, 820 N. French St., Wilmington 19801, (302)571-6262; fax (302)571-3862

U.S. Small Business Administration, 1 Rodney Square, 920 N. King St., Wilmington 19801, (302) 573-6295; fax (302)573-6060

Florida

City of Miami, Bureau of International Trade, 174 E. Flagler St., 7th Floor, Miami 33133, (305)579-3324

Florida Exporters and Importers Assn., P.O. Box 450648, Miami, FL 33145, (305)446-6646

U.S. Department of Commerce, US&FCS District Office, Federal Building, Suite 224, 51 S.W. First Ave., Miami 33130, (305)536-5267; fax (305)536-4765

Tampa Bay International Trade Council, P.O. Box 420, Tampa 33601, (813)228-7777

Tampa World Trade Council, International Department of the Greater Tampa Chamber of Commerce, P.O. Box 420, Tampa 33601, (813)228-7777

Georgia

Georgia Department of Agriculture, International Trade Div., 19 Martin Luther King Jr. Dr., Atlanta 30334, (404)656-3600

U.S. Department of Commerce, US&FCS District Office, 1365 Peachtree St. N.E., Suite 504, Atlanta 30309, (404)347-7000; fax (404)347-0108

U.S. Small Business Administration, 1720 Peachtree St. N.W., 6th Floor, Atlanta 30309, (404)881-4749

Hawaii

Hawaii Dept. of Business & Economic Development, Trade & Industrial Development, P.O. Box 2359, Honolulu 96804, (808)548-7719; fax (808)523-8637

U.S. Department of Commerce, US&FCS District Office, 4106 Federal Building, 300 Ala Monana Blvd., P.O. Box 50026, Honolulu 96850, (808)541-3435

Idaho

U.S. Department of Commerce, US&FCS District Office, 700 W. State St., 2nd Floor, Boise 83720, (208)334-3857; fax (208)334-2631

Illinois

American Assn. of Exporters and Importers, 7763 S. Kedzie Ave., Chicago 60652, (312)471-1958

Chicago Economic Development Commission, International Business Div., 20 N. Clark St., 28th Floor, Chicago 60602, (312)744-8666

U.S. Department of Commerce, US&FCS District Office, Mid-Continental Plaza Building, Room 1406, 55 E. Monroe St., Chicago 60603, (312)353-4450; fax (312)886-8025

Illinois Department of Business & Economic Development, 222 S. College St., Springfield 62706

Illinois Export Council, 214 State St., Springfield 62706, (217)782-7884

Indiana

Indiana Dept. of Commerce, International Trade Div., One N. Capitol, Suite 700, Indianapolis 46204-2248, (317)232-8846; fax (317)232-4146

Indiana Export Council, c/o U.S. Department of Commerce, Indiana Commerce Center, Suite 700, 1 N. Capitol, Indianapolis 46204, (317)269-6214

U.S. Department of Commerce, US&FCS District Office, One N. Capitol, Suite 520, Indianapolis 46204-2248, (317)226-6214; fax (317)226-6139

World Trade Club of Indiana, 1 N. Capitol, Suite 200, Indianapolis 46204-2248, (317)261-1169; fax (317)264-6855

Iowa

Iowa Department of Economic Development, International Trade, 200 E. Grand Ave., Des Moines 50309, (515)281-6785

U.S. Department of Commerce, US&FCS District Office, 817 Federal Building, 210 Walnut St., Des Moines 50309, (515)284-4222; fax (515)284-4021

Kansas

U.S. Department of Commerce, US&FCS District Office, River Park Place, Suite 580, 727 N. Waco St., Wichita 67203, (316)269-6160; fax (316)262-5652

U.S. Small Business Administration, 110 E. Waterman St., Wichita 67202, (316)269-6571

Kentucky

Kentuckiana World Commerce Council, P.O. Box 58456, Louisville 40258, (502)583-5551

Kentucky District Export Council, 601 W. Broadway Ave., Room 636-B, Louisville 40202, (502)582-5066

Help From Your Home State

U.S. Department of Commerce, US&FCS District Office, 601 W. Broadway Ave., Room 636-B, Louisville 40202, (502)582-5066; fax (502)582-6573

Louisiana

Louisiana Office of International Trade, Finance & Development, One Maritime Plaza, 101 France St., P.O. Box 44185, Baton Rouge 70804, (504)342-4320; fax (504)342-5389

Louisiana Department of Commerce, International Trade & Investment, 343 International Trade Mart, New Orleans 70130, (504)568-5255

U.S. Department of Commerce, US&FCS District Office, 432 International Trade Mart, 2 Canal St., New Orleans 70130, (504)589-6546; fax (504)589-2337

Maine

Main Development Office, International Trade, State House, Station 59, Augusta 04333, (207)289-5700; fax (207)289-2861

Maine World Trade Assn., 77 Sewall St., Augusta 04330, (207)622-0234; fax (207)622-3760

U.S. Department of Commerce, US&FCS District Office, 77 Sewall St., Augusta 04330, (207)622-8249

Maryland

U.S. Department of Commerce, US&FCS District Office, 413 U.S. Customhouse, Gay & Lombard Sts., Baltimore 21202, (301)962-3560; fax (301)962-7813

Massachusetts

International Business Center of New England, 470 Atlantic Ave., Boston 02210, (617)542-0426

Massachusetts Commission on International Trade & Foreign Investment, State House, Suite 413F, Boston 02133, (617)722-1673

Office of International Trade, 100 Cambridge St., Room 902, Boston 02202, (617)367-1830; fax (617)227-3488

Michigan

Michigan District Export Council, 445 Federal Building, Detroit 48226, (313)226-3650

U.S. Department of Commerce, US&FCS District Office, 1140 McNamara Building, 477 Michigan Ave., Detroit 48226, (313)226-3650; fax (313)226-3657

U.S. Small Business Administration, 515 Patrick V. McNamara Building, 477 Michigan Ave., Room 515, Detroit 48226, (313)226-6075

Michigan State Chamber of Commerce, Small Business Programs, 200 N. Washington Square, Suite 400, Lansing 48933, (517)371-2100

World Trade Services, Ottawa Building North, 4th Floor, P.O. Box 30017, Lansing 48909, (517)373-1054; fax (517)335-4607

Minnesota

Greater Minneapolis Chamber of Commerce, 15 S. Fifth St., Minneapolis 55402, (612)339-8521

Minnesota World Trade Assn., 5235 Xerxes Ave. South, Minneapolis 55410, (612)926-6202

U.S. Department of Commerce, US&FCS District Office, 108 Federal Building, 110 S. 4th St., Minneapolis 55401, (612)348-1638; fax (612)348-1650

Governor's Special Trade Representative, Minnesota Trade Office, 90 W. Plato Blvd., St. Paul 55107, (612)297-4222

Mississippi

International Trade Club of Mississippi, P.O. Box 16673, Jackson 39236, (601)981-7906

U.S. Department of Commerce, US&FCS District Office, 300 Woodrow Wilson Blvd., Suite 328, Jackson 39213, (601)965-4388; fax (601)965-5386

Missouri

Missouri Department of Agriculture, International Marketing Div., P.O. Box 630, Jefferson City 65102, (314)751-5611

Missouri Department of Commerce & Economic Development, International Business Development, 301 W. High St., Jefferson City 65101, (314) 751-4855; fax (314)634-5472

International Trade Club of Greater Kansas City, 920 Main St., Suite 600, Kansas City 64105, (816)221-1460

U.S. Department of Commerce, US&FCS District Office, 601 E. 12th St., Room 635, Kansas City 64106, (816)426-3141; fax (816)426-3140

Montana

International Business Program, College of Business, Montana State University, Bozeman 59717, (406)994-6188; fax (406)994-6206

Montana Department of Commerce, International Trade Office, State Capitol, Helena 59620, (406)444-3923

Nebraska

Midwest International Trade Assn., P.O. Box 1434, Downtown Station, Omaha 68101

U.S. Department of Commerce, US&FCS District Office, 11133 O St., Omaha 68101

Nevada

Nevada Department of Economic Development, Capitol Complex, Carson City 89710, (702)687-4325; fax (702)687-4450

U.S. Small Business Administration, 301 E. Steward St., Las Vegas 89125, (702)385-6611

New Hampshire

New Hampshire Department of Resources & Economic Development, Foreign Trade & Commercial Development, 105 Loudon Rd., Building 2, Concord 03301, (603)271-2591; fax (603)271-2629

U.S. Small Business Administration, 60 Park Pl., 4th Floor, Newark 07102, (201)645-2434

World Trade Assn. of New Jersey, 5 Commerce St., Newark 07102, (201)623-7070

New Mexico

U.S. Department of Commerce, US&FCS District Office, 625 Silver Ave. S.W., Suite 320, Albuquerque 87102, (505)766-2070; fax (505)766-1057

New York

Buffalo Area Chamber of Commerce, Economic Development Dept., 107 Delaware Ave., Buffalo 14202, (716)849-6677

U.S. Department of Commerce, US&FCS District Office, 1312 Federal Building, 111 W. Huron St., Buffalo 14202, (716)846-4191; fax (716)846-5290

American Management Assn., International Div., 135 W. 50th St., New York 10020, (212)586-8100

National Assn. of Export Companies, 200 Madison Ave., New York 10016, (212)561-2025

Help From Your Home State 137

National Customs Brokers & Forwarders Assn. of America, One World Trade Center, Room 1109, New York 10048, (212)432-0050

New York State Department of Commerce, International Div., 230 Park Ave., New York 10169, (212)309-0502

U.S. Council of the International Chamber of Commerce, 1212 Avenue of the Americas, New York 10036, (212)354-4480

World Trade Institute, One World Trade Center, New York 10048, (212)466-4044

U.S. Department of Commerce, 121 East Ave., Rochester 14604, (716)263-6480

World Commerce Assn. of Central New York, 1700 One Mony Plaza, 100 Madison Ave., Syracuse 13202, (315)422-1343

North Carolina

U.S. Department of Commerce, US&FCS District Office, 203 Federal Building, 324 W. Market St., P.O. Box 1950, Greensboro 27402, (919)333-5354; fax (919)333-5158

North Carolina State University, International Trade Center, P.O. Box 5125, Raleigh 27650, (919)737-7912

North Dakota

North Dakota Economic Development Commission, International Trade Div., 1050 E. Interstate Ave., Bismarck 58505, (701)224-2810
Ohio

Ohio

Greater Cincinnati World Trade Club, 120 W. 5th St., Cincinnati 45202, (513)579-3122

Southern Ohio District Export Council, 9504 Federal Building, 550 Main St., Cincinnati 45202, (513)684-2944

U.S. Department of Commerce, US&FCS District Office, 9504 Federal Building, 550 Main St., Cincinnati 45202, (513)684-2944; fax (513)684-3200

Cleveland World Trade Assn., 690 Huntington Building, Cleveland 44115, (216)621-3300

Greater Cleveland Growth Assn., International Div., 690 Union Commerce Building, Cleveland 44115, (216)621-3300

Northern Ohio District Export Council, Plaza Nine Building, 55 Erieview Plaza, Suite 700, Cleveland 44114, (216)522-4750

Ohio Department of Development, International Trade Division, 77 S. High St., Columbus 43266-0101, (614)466-5017; fax (614)463-1540

International Trade Institute, 5055 N. Main St., Dayton 45415, (513)276-5995

Toledo Area International Trade Assn., 218 Huron St., Toledo 43604, (419)243-8191

Oklahoma

Oklahoma City International Trade Club, Oklahoma City Chamber of Commerce, One Santa Fe Plaza, Oklahoma City 73102, (405)232-6381

Oklahoma Department of Economic Development, International Trade Div., 4024 N. Lincoln Blvd., P.O. Box 53424, Oklahoma City 73152, (405)521-3501

U.S. Department of Commerce, US&FCS District Office, P.O. Box 26980, Oklahoma City 73126-0980, (405)231-5302; fax (405)841-5199

Tulsa World Trade Assn., 1821 N. 106th East Ave., Tulsa 74116, (918)836-0338

U.S. Department of Commerce, 440 S. Houston St., Suite 505, Tulsa 74127, (918)581-7650; fax (918)581-2844

Oregon

Institute for International Trade & Commerce, Portland State University, 1912 S.W. 6th Ave., Room 260, Portland 97207, (503)229-3246

Oregon Department of Economic Development, International Trade Div., One World Trade Center, Suite 300, 121 S.W. Salmon St., Portland 97204, (503)229-5625 or toll-free (800)452-7813; fax (503)222-5050

Pacific Northwest International Trade Assn., 200 S.W. Market, Suite 220, Portland 97201, (503)228-4361

U.S. Department of Commerce, US&FCS District Office, One World Trade Center, Suite 242, 121 S.W. Salmon St., Portland 97204, (503)326-3001; fax (503)326-6351

Pennsylvania

Pennsylvania Department of Commerce, Bureau of Export Trade, Forum Building, Room 463, Harrisburg 17120, (717)787-7190; fax (717)234-4560

Assessment of International Markets Program, University of Pittsburgh, Pittsburgh 15260, (412) 624-1777

International Trade Executives Club of Pittsburgh, 2002 Federal Building, 1000 Liberty Ave., Pittsburgh 15222, (412)644-2850

U.S. Department of Commerce, US&FCS District Office, 2002 Federal Building, 1000 Liberty Ave., Pittsburgh 15222, (412)644-2850; fax (412)644-4875

Western Pennsylvania District Export Council, 1000 Liberty Ave., Room 2002, Pittsburgh 15222, (412)644-2850

Puerto Rico

Puerto Rico Department of Commerce, P.O. Box 4275, San Juan 00905, (809)721-3290

Puerto Rico Economic Development Administration, GPO Box 2350, San Juan 00936, (809)758-4747

Rhode Island

U.S. Department of Commerce, US&FCS District Office, 7 Jackson Walkway, Providence 02903, (401)528-5104; fax (401)528-5067

World Trade Center, Greater Providence Chamber of Commerce, Howard Building, 10 Dorrance St., Providence 02903, (401)521-5000

South Carolina

U.S. Department of Commerce, 17 Lockwood Dr., Charleston 29401, (803)724-4361

U.S. Department of Commerce, US&FCS District Office, Strom Thurmond Federal Building, Suite 172, 1835 Assembly St., Columbia 29201, (803)765-5345; fax (803)253-3614

South Dakota

Governor's Office of Economic Development, 711 Wells Ave., Pierre 57501-3335, (605)773-5032; fax (605)773-3256

Tennessee

Mid-South Exporters' Roundtable, P.O. Box 3521, Memphis 38103, (901)761-3490

U.S. Department of Commerce, US&FCS District Office, 3876 Central Ave., P.O. Box 224, Memphis 38111, (901)521-4826; fax (901)575-3510

Middle Tennessee World Trade Council, P.O. Box 17367, Nashville 37202, (615)329-4931

Tennessee Department of Economic & Community Development, Export Promotion Office, Andrew Jackson State Building, Room 10, 320 6th Ave., 7th Floor, Nashville 37219, (615)741-5870; telex 5551 96 ECD NAS

Texas

Texas Department of Commerce, Office of International Trade, P.O. Box 12728, Capitol Station, Austin 78711, (512)320-9439; fax (512)320-9674

Texas Economic Development Commission, International Trade Dept., P.O. Box 13561, Austin 78711, (512)472-5059

Texas Industrial Commission, International Trade Div., 712 Sam Houston State Office Building, Box 12728, Capitol Station, Austin 78711, (512)475-5551

Center for International Business, World Trade Center, Suite 184, P.O. Box 58428, Dallas 75258, (214)742-7301

International Trade Assn. of Dallas, Box 672, Dallas 75221, (214) 658-6323 or (214)369-5825

Texas International Business Assn., P.O. Box 29334, Dallas 75229, (214) 692-1214

U.S. Department of Commerce, US&FCS District Office, 1100 Commerce St., Room 7A5, Dallas 75242, (214)767-0543; fax (214)767-8240

U.S. Small Business Administration, 4100 Rio Bravo, Suite 300, El Paso 79902, (915)543-7586

Fort Worth Export-Import Club, Box 17372, Fort Worth 76102, (817)625-2211

Houston World Trade Assn., 1520 Texas Ave., Suite 239, Houston 77002, (713) 225-0967

U.S. Department of Commerce, US&FCS District Office, 2625 Federal Courthouse, 515 Rusk St., Houston 77002, (713)229-2578; fax (713)229-2203

Export-Import Club of San Antonio, 221 Olmos Dr. West, San Antonio 78212, (512)826-3400

U.S. Small Business Administration, 727 E. Duranyo St., Room A-513, San Antonio 78206, (512)229-6250

Utah

U.S. Department of Commerce, US&FCS District Office, U.S. Post Office Building, Room 340, 350 S. Main St., Salt Lake City 84101, (801)524-5116; fax (801)524-5886

World Trade Assn. of Utah, 10 Exchange Pl., Suite 301-302, Salt Lake City 84111, (801)531-1515

Vermont

Vermont-Canadian Free Trade Office, 7 Burlington Square, Suite 600, Burlington 05401, (802)865-0777; fax (802)658-7862

U.S. Small Business Administration, 87 State St., Room 204, Montpelier 05602, (802)229-0538

Virginia

VESTRAC/Export Trading Co. of Virginia Port Authority, 600 World Trade Center, Norfolk 23510, (804)623-8000

Virginia Department of World Trade, 6000 World Trade Center, Norfolk 23510, (800)553-3170; fax (804)683-2948

U.S. Department of Commerce, US&FCS District Office, 8010 Federal Building, 400 N. 8th St., Richmond 23240, (804)771-2246; fax (804)771-2390

Virginia District Export Council, P.O. Box 10190, Richmond 23240, (804)771-2246

Virginia Div. of Industrial Development, International Trade & Development Dept., 1010 State Office Building, Richmond 23219, (804)786-4486

Washington

Washington Council on International Trade, Fourth & Vine Building, Suite 420, Seattle 98121, (206)621-8485

Washington Department of Trade & Economic Development, 2001 Sixth Ave., Suite 2600, Seattle 89121, (206)464-7143; fax (206)464-7222

Washington State International Trade Fair, 312 First Ave. North, Seattle 98109, (206)682-6911

West Virginia

U.S. Department of Commerce, US&FCS District Office, 3402 New Federal Office Building, 500 Quarrier St., Charleston 25301, (304)347-5123; fax (304)347-5408

West Virginia District Export Council, P.O. Box 26, Charleston 25321, (304)343-8874

Wisconsin

Wisconsin Department of Business Development, 123 W. Washington Ave., Room 650, Madison 53702, (608)266-3222

U.S. Department of Commerce, US&FCS District Office, 606 Federal Building, 517 E. Wisconsin Ave., Milwaukee 53202, (414)297-3473; fax (414)297-3470

Wisconsin World Trade Center, 424 E. Wisconsin Ave., Milwaukee 53202, (414)274-3840; fax (414)274-3846

World Trade Assn. of Milwaukee, 828 N. Broadway Ave., Room 310, Milwaukee 53202, (414)273-3000

Wyoming

International Business Officer, Office of the Governor, Herschler Building, 2nd Floor East, Cheyenne 82002, (307)777-7574

International Trade Office, Herschler Building, 2nd Floor West, Cheyenne 82002, (307)777-6412; fax (307)777-5840

CHAPTER 9

UNCLE SAM WILL HELP, TOO

If your home state is interested in seeing you become successful in export, the U.S. government is even more so. This chapter provides you with the information and resources you will need to get started.

Whether provided by a public or private organization, a great deal of assistance is available—and much of it is free or is offered at a minimal cost. The trick is in knowing how and where to find it.

Various reference works will get you started:

- The U.S. Department of Commerce provides a free US&FCS counseling kit that contains information on Matchmaker trade missions, commercial news, and catalog and videotape catalog programs. It also publishes the free *How to Get the Most From Overseas Exhibitions*. Contact: U.S. Department of Commerce, US&FCS, Room H 2116, Washington D.C. 20230, (800)343-4300, Operator 940.

- The U.S. Small Business Administration has produced *Market Overseas with U.S. Government Help* (Management Aids

145

#7.003), *The World Is Your Market*, and *International Trade Assistance* (SBA Fact Sheet #42). Contact: U.S. Small Business Administration, Office of International Trade, 1441 L St. N.W., Suite 501A, Washington, D.C. 20416, (202)653-7794.

- The Agency for International Development offers three free publications that are very helpful: *Facts About AID*, which describes the agency's foreign aid program; *Export Opportunities with the Agency for International Development*; and *AID Importer List*, which catalogs importers interested in introducing American products to selected AID-recipient countries. Contact: Agency for International Development, Washington D.C. 20523-1414, (202)647-1850.

- Representative of the information available through a variety of non-government organizations, the U.S. Chamber of Commerce offers a free publication, *How To Expand Your Market Through Exporting* (Pub. #2004). Contact: U.S. Chamber of Commerce of the United States, Publications Fulfillment, 1610 H St. N.W., Washington, D.C. 20062, (202)659-6000.

You can also contact your nearest Federal Information Center for even more assistance:

Alabama
  (To write, address the Atlanta, GA office)
  Birmingham: (205)322-8591
  Mobile: (205)438-1421

Alaska
  Anchorage: 701 C. St., Box 33, Anchorage 99513, (907)271-3650

Arizona
  (To write, address the San Diego, CA office)
  Phoenix: (602)261-3313

Arkansas
(To write, address the Fort Worth, TX office)
Little Rock: (501)378-6177

California
Los Angeles: 300 N. Los Angeles St., Los Angeles 90012, (213)688-3800
Sacramento: 650 Capitol Mall, Sacramento 95814, (916)440-3344
San Diego: Government Information Center, 880 Front St., San Diego 92188, (619)293-6030
San Francisco: 450 Golden Gate Ave., Box 36082, San Francisco 94102, (415)556-6600
Santa Ana: (714)836-2386

Colorado
Colorado Springs: (303)471-9491
Denver: Federal Center, P.O. Box 25006, Denver 80225, (303)236-7181
Pueblo: (303)544-9523

Connecticut
(To write, address the New York, NY office)
Hartford: (203)527-2617
New Haven: (203)624-4720

Florida
Ft. Lauderdale: (305)522-8531
Jacksonville: (904)354-4756
Miami: (305)350-4155
Orlando: (305)422-1800
St. Petersburg: 144 First Ave. South, Room 105, St. Petersburg 33701, (813)893-3495
Tampa: (813)229-7911
West Palm Beach: (305)833-7566

Georgia
Atlanta: 75 Spring St. N.W., Atlanta 30303, (404)221-6891

Hawaii
   Honolulu: 300 Ala Moana Blvd., Box 50091, Honolulu 96850, (808)546-8620

Illinois
   Chicago: 230 S. Dearborn St., 33rd Floor, Chicago 60604, (312)353-4242

Indiana
   (To write, address the Cincinnati, OH office)
   Gary: (219)883-4110
   Indianapolis: (317)269-7373

Iowa
   To write, address the Omaha, NE office or call toll-free (800)532-1556

Kansas
   To write, address the St. Louis, MO office or call toll-free (800)432-2934

Kentucky
   (To write, address the Cincinnati, OH office)
   Louisville: (502)582-6261

Louisiana
   (To write, address the Houston, TX office)
   New Orleans: (504)589-6696

Maryland
   (To write, address the Philadelphia, PA office)
   Baltimore: (301)962-4980

Massachusetts
   Boston: McCormack P.O.C.H. Building, Room 812, Boston 02109, (617)223-7121

Michigan
   Detroit: 477 Michigan Ave., Room M-25, Detroit 48226, (313)226-7016
   Grand Rapids: (616)451-2628

Minnesota
   (To write, address the Chicago, IL office)
   Minneapolis: (612)349-5333

Missouri
   St. Louis: 1520 Market St., Room 2616, St. Louis 63103, (314)425-4106
   Toll-free from all other cities in Missouri: (800)392-7711

Nebraska
   Omaha: 215 N. 17th St., Omaha 68102, (402)221-3353
   Toll-free from all other cities in Nebraska: (800)642-8383

New Jersey
   (Northern New Jersey, write to the New York, NY office; southern New Jersey, write to the Philadelphia, PA office)
   Newark: (201)645-3600
   Trenton: (609)396-4400

New Mexico
   (To write, address the Fort worth, TX office)
   Albuquerque: (505)766-3091

New York
   Albany: (518)463-4421
   Buffalo: 111 W. Huron St., Buffalo 14202, (716)846-4010
   New York: 26 Federal Plaza, Room 2-110, New York 10278, (212)264-4464
   Rochester: (716)546-5075
   Syracuse: (315)476-8545

North Carolina
  (To write, address the Atlanta, GA office)
  Charlotte: (704)376-3600

Ohio
  Akron: (216)375-5638
  Cincinnati: 550 Main St., Room 7411, Cincinnati 45202, (513)684-2801
  Cleveland: (216)522-4040
  Columbus: (614)221-1014
  Dayton: (513)223-7377
  Toledo: (419)241-3223

Oklahoma
  (To write, address the Fort Worth, TX office)
  Oklahoma City: (415)231-4868
  Tulsa: (918)584-4193

Oregon
  Portland: 1220 S.W. Third Ave., Room 318, Portland 97204, (503)221-2222

Pennsylvania
  Philadelphia: 600 Arch St., Room 1232, Philadelphia 19106, (215)597-7042
  Pittsburgh: (412)644-3456

Rhode Island
  (To write, address the Boston, MA office)
  Providence: (401)331-5565

Tennessee
  (To write, address the Atlanta, GA office)
  Chattanooga: (615)265-8231
  Memphis: (901)521-3285
  Nashville: (615)242-5056

Texas
  Austin: (512)472-5494
  Dallas: (214)767-8585
  Fort Worth: 819 Taylor St., Fort Worth 76102, (817)334-3624
  Houston: 515 Rusk Ave., Houston 77002, (713)229-2552
  San Antonio: (512)224-4471

Utah
  (To write, address the Denver, CO office)
  Salt Lake City: (801)524-5353

Virginia
  (To write, address the Philadelphia, PA office)
  Norfolk: (804)441-3101
  Richmond: (804)643-4928
  Roanoke: (703)982-8591

Washington
  (To write, address the Portland, OR office)
  Seattle: (206)442-0570
  Tacoma: (206)383-5230

Wisconsin
  (To write, address the Chicago, IL office)
  Milwaukee: (414)271-2273

U.S. Department Of Commerce

No government agency offers a greater variety of services related to export—or provides greater ease of access—than the U.S. Department of Commerce.

If you are interested in entering the export field, expanding your export sales, locating an overseas agent or distributor, or licensing a product for manufacture abroad, either the Department's International Trade Administration (ITA) or its National Oceanic & Atmospheric Administration (NOAA) probably can help you. These agencies help businesses learn about opportunities to exhibit, promote, and sell their products overseas; keep abreast of marketing, economic, governmental, and other meaningful trends abroad; stage overseas exhibitions; and meet foreign buyers.

The ITA organizes its services according to industry sectors—capital goods, consumer goods, and so on. To help you find offshore buyers for your goods or services, it offers:

- *Export Contact List Service*—a listing of foreign importers, agents distributors, customers, manufacturers, service organizations, retailers, and end users.

- *Export Mailing List Service*—a means of producing lists by commodity classification.

- *Trade Lists*—names of controlled trading companies where state-controlled organizations conduct foreign trade; or firms in selected developing countries.

- *Agent/Distributor Service*—up to six names of firms that are qualified to represent you abroad.

- *Trade Opportunities Program*—Provides information on opportunities for direct sales to foreign buyers, both private and governmental, and notices of foreign companies offering to represent U.S. companies overseas.

- *Export Statistics Profiles*—tables showing U.S. exports within a specific industry help to locate the best export markets by analyzing the industry's exports product-by-product and country-by-country for a five-year period; $70 per profile.

- *Annual Worldwide Industry Reviews*—combination country-by-country market assessments, export trends, and five-year statistical tables for a single industry. Each covers from eight to eighteen countries; one report, $200; two reports, $350; three reports within the same industry, $500.

- *World Traders Data Reports*—business reports prepared by U.S. Foreign Commerce Service posts abroad list trader's type of organization, year established, relative size, number of employees, general reputation, and related data.

The Department of Commerce produces several publications. *Business America* reports every two weeks on international markets, economic conditions, and specific sales opportunities. *Commerce Business Daily* summarizes U.S. government procurement invitations, subcontracting leads, contract awards, sales of surplus property, and foreign business opportunities. *Overseas Business Reports* examine marketing factors, trade regulations, economic data, selling practices, and market profiles of individual countries. *Foreign Economic Trends and Their Implications for the U.S.* also reports on individual countries, providing information on current business conditions, current and near-term prospects, growth, and buying patterns.

Global Market Surveys are country market summaries that indicate the sales potential of a target industry's product in a number of growth markets. *Market Share Reports* contain statistical data on imports of more than 1,000 commodities by eighty-eight countries over a five-year span.

The ITA also publishes several useful brochures including *A Guide to Financing Exports, A Basic Guide to Exporting, The EMC—Your Export Department, Product Marketing Service, Business Services Checklist,* and *Publications for Business from ITA.*

The Department of Commerce also offers: trade missions; exhibitions at which ITA sponsors exporter participation in major international shows; solo exhibitions of U.S. products that are sponsored by ITA whenever suitable international trade fairs are not available; exhibitions at Export Development Offices concentrating on specific product categories and displaying only U.S. products; catalog shows disseminating U.S. product catalogs, sales brochures, and other sales literature at trade shows, U.S. Embassies, and U.S. Consulates; product marketing service—temporary bases of operation at nine U.S. Export Development Offices for U.S. business personnel traveling overseas. These offices help to identify prime prospects, arrange appointments, counsel you on doing business in that country, and locate a secretary or interpreter. The Department also offers a new product information service that takes your product information and sends it abroad to U.S. Embassies and U.S. Consulates, where it is translated and distributed.

The ITA can also advise a company about using an export managing company (EMC) or an export trading company. EMCs provide most of the services required for successful foreign trade and they charge a fee or a percentage for their services. An export trading company, on the other hand, is formed by several companies who use it to pool their needs for export services. Export trading companies operate under a 1982 law, but must also be careful not to violate state or federal antitrust laws.

A foreign trade zone, a domestic location legally outside of customs jurisdiction, is yet another option. In such zones, companies may store, assemble, inspect, repack, and perform a variety of other activities that otherwise would have to be done overseas due to customs regulations. For export operations, such zones provide accelerated export status for excise tax rebates and customs drawbacks.

Foreign trade zones have existed since 1934, and there are now some 150 general-purpose zones and 140 subzones in operation in the U.S. More zones are being created constantly.

Foreign trade zones also exist in other countries, such as the Dominican Republic, Mexico, South Korea, Hong Kong, Malaysia, Mauritius, and Ireland, among others. Over 70 percent of the 2,100 companies now using foreign trade zones are small- to medium-sized businesses.

There are a number of things to keep in mind when deciding whether to locate in a foreign trade zone and, if so, which one: restrictions on duty-free imports of raw materials and unfinished goods needed in the production process; salaries, degree of sophistication, and size of the local workforce; available production facilities, including electricity and water, warehouse facilities, and room for expansion; availability of suppliers and subcontractors; transportation facilities; the host country's tax policies, including whether there would be a duty charged on production equipment

Uncle Sam Will Help, Too 155

and other machinery that might have to be imported; financial incentives offered by the host country, including loans, grants, subsidies, and tax deferrals; the economic and political stability of the host country.

Generally speaking, you will want to select a foreign trade zone that is nearest to your own facilities, the facilities of your largest customer, or your largest market. To locate zones in the region of interest to you, contact National Association of Foreign Trade Zones, International Square, Suite 400, 1825 I St. NW, Washington, D.C. 20006; (202)429-2020. For additional information on these zones, contact the Foreign Trade Zones Board, U.S. Department of Commerce, Washington D.C. 20230, or any ITA field office.

The National Marine Fisheries Service (NMES) is involved in the export of seafood products and offers a variety of helpful programs and services, including identifying potential foreign markets; information on tariff and non-tariff barriers; information on foreign seafood import regulations; information on foreign consumer preferences in seafood; inspection services to ensure that U.S. products meet foreign import standards; overseas trade opportunity data via the Computer Assisted System for the Export of Seafood (CASES); U.S. seafood sales missions overseas; and U.S. seafood sales exhibitions at international food shows. For additional information on these activities, contact National Marine Fisheries Service, NOAA, U.S. Department of Commerce, Washington, D.C. 20235; (202)634-7451.

For those specifically interested in the European Community, an interagency study group has been formed to assist them. It is composed of specialists in the following areas who are responsible to the U.S. Trade Representative appointed by the President.

U.S. & Foreign Commerce Service (US&FCS)

The US&FCS is supported by 1,100 experienced professionals working in sixty-seven U.S. cities and 126 foreign countries. Contact them at:

Export Counseling Center   Room 1066   (202)377-3181
Export Promotion Services   P.O. Box 14207   (202)377-2432
  Office of Information   Washington, DC
  Product Development & Distribution 20044
Office of Market Programs   Room 2116   (202)377-4231
Information on export-related   (202)377-5367
  publications
Office of Foreign Operations
  Africa, Near East & South Asia   Room 3104   (202)377-2736
East Asia & Pacific   Room 3104   (202)377-2736
Europe   Room 3122   (202)377-1599
Western Hemisphere   Room 3122   (202)377-1599

Trade Administration

Exporter's Service (export licensing, controls, etc.)   Room 1099   (202)377-4811
Office of Antiboycott Compliance   Room 3886   (202)377-2381

Minority Business Development Agency

Minority Export Development   Room 5093   (202)377-2881
  Consulting Program

For information regarding specific industry sectors, contact the appropriate product/service specialist:

Trade Development

Product/Service Specialist
Aerospace   Room 6877   (202)377-8228
Automotive & Consumer Goods   Room 4324   (202)377-0823
Basic Industries   Room 4045   (202)377-0614
Capital Goods & International   Room 2001-B   (202)377-5023
  Construction
Export Trading Company Affairs   Room 5618   (202)377-5131
International Major Projects   Room 2007   (202)377-5225
Science & Electronics   Room 1001-A   (202)377-4466
Services   Room 1128   (202)377-5261
Textiles & Apparel   Room 3100   (202)377-3737
Trade Information & Analysis   Room 3814-B   (202)377-1316

U.S. Department of Agriculture

The Foreign Agriculture Service (FAS) of the Department of Agriculture provides a wide range of export services. Overseas, the Department maintains a network of agricultural counselors, attachés, and trade officers; at home, a team of commodity analysts, marketing specialists, and other staff personnel.

The Agricultural counselors and attachés supervise market development activities and alert U.S. exporters to foreign market opportunities and competitive activities. This staff is responsible for covering over 100 overseas countries.

FAS programs include:

- *Agricultural Information & Marketing Services (AIMS)*—A liaison between U.S. suppliers and foreign buyers, AIMS provides agricultural data, trade leads, relevant trade information, and marketing services such as product publicity, international marketing profiles, and foreign importer listings.

- *AIMS Direct Mail Service*—Specializes in helping exporters respond to foreign trade inquiries for specific agricultural products. Leads generally are forwarded to exporters within forty-eight hours of the time the information is received in Washington.

- *AIMS Export Briefs*—A weekly trade letter, this service contains all trade inquiries received by FAS headquarters during the week, plus news of trade shows and data on trade developments.

Agricultural Trade Offices operate in London, Hamburg, Beijing, Singapore, Seoul, Tunis, Bahrain, Warsaw, Lagos, Caracas, and Jidda to provide services for exporters and space for small product displays. They also arrange product demonstrations for potential customers.

New exporters can advertise their products free of charge in *Contacts for U.S. Farm Products*, a newsletter sent to FAS agricultural representatives overseas, who in turn distribute the information to the areas for which they are responsible.

FAS also assists at overseas trade fair exhibits, hotel restaurant institutional exhibits, international food shows, agent food exhibits, agricultural attaché product displays, and livestock shows. It also aids with point-of-purchase promotions.

Regional Contacts

Regional groups work with the exporter and FAS to develop a three-year product promotional program. There are four of these regional groups:

Eastern U.S. Agricultural & Food Export Council, 2 World Trade Center, Suite 5082, New York, NY 10047, (212)432-0020, telex 420859 EUSAFEC
  Services: Connecticut, Delaware, Maine, New Hampshire, New Jersey, New York, Pennsylvania, Rhode Island, Vermont.

Southern U.S. Trade Assn., International Trade Mart, 2 Canal St., Suite 338, New Orleans, LA 70130, (504)568-5986, telex 584319 SUSTA NLN
  Services: Alabama, Arkansas, Florida, Georgia, Kentucky, Louisiana, Maryland, Mississippi, North Carolina, Puerto Rico, Oklahoma, South Carolina, Tennessee, Texas, Virginia, West Virginia.

Mid-America International Agri-Trade Council, 300 W. Washington St., Suite 1001, Chicago, IL 60606, (312)368-4448, TWX (910)221-5686
  Services: Illinois, Indiana, Iowa, Kansas, Michigan, Minnesota, Missouri, Nebraska, North Dakota, Ohio, South Dakota, Wisconsin.

Western U.S. Agricultural Trade Assn., 13101 N.E. Highway 99, Suite 200, Vancouver, WA 98665, (206)574-2624

Services: Alaska, California, Hawaii, New Mexico, Oregon, Washington, Utah, Wyoming, American Samoa, Guam.

Through the regional cooperator groups, FAS operates the Value-Added Promotion Program which assists processors, packers, manufacturers, distributors, export agents, wholesalers, export trading companies, and others to promote their products in specific markets.

The FAS encourages firms to export their products by reimbursing them for a portion of their export promotional expenses via the Export Incentive Program.

For detailed information on FAS programs related to minority businesses or small business, contact the Coordinator for Minority & Small Business Programs, Export Programs Div., (202)475-3418.

For specific commodity categories, FAS has six divisions:

Dairy, Livestock & Poultry Div.	(202)447-8031
Grain & Feed Div.	(202)447-6219
Horticulture & Tropical Products Div.	(202)447-6590
Oilseeds & Products Div.	(202)447-7037
Tobacco, Cotton & Seed Div.	(202)382-9516
Forest Products Div.	(202)382-8138

Write to the U.S. Department of Agriculture, 14th St. & Independence Ave. S.W., Washington, D.C. 20250.

U.S. Small Business Administration

Working with the Department of Commerce and other organizations, the Small Business Administration co-sponsors export workshops.

Financial assistance can be obtained in the form of loans and loan guarantees for equipment, facilities, materials, working capital, and specific export market development activities.

The agency's *Export Information System Data Reports* are available for 1,700 SITC product categories. These reports provide businesses with a list of 25 of the largest import markets for their produce and the ten best markets for exports of those products. They also provide information on trends and the major sources of foreign competition.

The SBA will pay the participation fee for a limited number of small businesses to engage in specific international trade shows and trade missions.

SBA publications include *Is Exporting for You?* and *Fact Sheets #42* and *#51*, which describe export and related services. Both are free.

Write to the U.S. Small Business Administration, Office of International Trade, 1441 L St. NW, Washington, D.C. 20416, (202)653-7794.

Agency For International Development (AID)

This federal agency administers most of the foreign economic assistance programs and has field representatives in about sixty countries throughout Africa, Latin America, Asia, and the Near East. Some of its programs enable U.S. businesses to compete for the sale of goods and technical services that the agency provides to underdeveloped countries.

The agency has two types of programs in which U.S. firms may participate:

- Commodity Import Programs finance the procurement of a wide range of basic commodities needed in developing countries. Under this program, funds are allocated by the foreign government to its various ministries and in the private sector to provide the foreign exchange that is needed to buy such items as machinery, industrial chemicals, tallow, farm equipment, and medical supplies.

- Commodities bought as a part of project procurements are related to project loans or grants financing specific facilities and undertakings, such as construction of irrigation facilities, rural health networks, malaria control programs, or equipping small farmers with needed tools and machinery.

Loans and grants from the agency also are used to finance the services of consultants in agriculture, rural development, nutrition, health, population planning, education, human resources, housing, and private sector development. At times AID acts on behalf of the foreign country and acts as the prime contractor in hiring technical experts. In such cases, AID frequently restricts competition for technical services through small business set-asides and the Small Business Administration's 8(a) Program.

AID's Office of Small and Disadvantaged Business Utilitization has developed a computerized system that links U.S. suppliers of manufactured goods with foreign buyers. This system, the Automated Supplier System for Export Trade (ASSET), was created in 1983 and provides information on where to obtain goods produced by small- and medium-sized U.S. businesses that are independent, disadvantaged, and minority-owned.

Write to the Agency for International Development, Department of State Building, 320 21st NW, Washington, D.C. 20523; (202)235-1840.

Federal Laboratory Consortium For Technology Transfer

The U.S. operates 400 national laboratories employing some 200,000 scientists and engineers. From these laboratories pours a steady stream of new technology—and it is available to you. Federal laboratories have been given a mandate to share their technology with the private sector. The Federal Laboratory Consortium for Technology Transfer has been designated to serve as the clearinghouse.

For information, write Center of the Utilization of Federal Technology, U.S. Department of Commerce, Washington, D.C. 20230.

U.S. International Trade Commission

The U.S. International Trade Commission has broad powers to study all factors relating to U.S. foreign trade; their effect on domestic production, employment and consumption; and the competitiveness of U.S. made products.

The International Trade Commission investigates broad trade issues. It also investigates trends in world production and trade. Occasionally, it issues reports on such subjects as industry targeting and its effect on U.S. industries.

When a product is being imported to the United States in such quantities as to threaten a competing American industry, the Commission may conduct an investigation and, if relief is considered warranted, advise the President to increase duties or establish import quotas.

Another area for investigation by the Commission is the one of unfair competition, such as the violation of patents, copyrights or trademarks. When such practices are found to exist, the Commission may order the offender to cease-and-desist or even order such products to be denied entry to the U.S.

Other areas of concern to the Commission include imports that are subsidized or are sold at less than fair value, and issues involving tariffs.

Like many other federal agencies, the International Trade Commission is organized into industry divisions:

Agriculture, Fisheries & Forest Products
Textiles, Leather Products & Apparel
Energy & Chemicals
Machinery & Equipment
Minerals & Metals
General Manufactures

Write to U.S. International Trade Commission, 500 E St. SW, Washington, D.C. 20436; (202)252-1000 or (800)343-9822, telex (710)822-9507, fax 252-1798.

U.S. Customs Service

If a company needs assistance in a foreign country, it may discover that there is a U.S. Customs attaché or senior representative there.

Uncle Sam Will Help, Too   163

Since the service is constantly being modified, the following list already may be outdated ... but it will serve as a guide:

Canada
Senior Customs Representative, U.S. Consulate, Rour du Sud, Suite 1122, Complex des Jardins, Montreal 45B 1G1 P.Q., 281-1456

England
Customs Attaché, American Embassy, Room G94, 24/32 Grosvenor Square, London W.1, England, 499-1212.

France
Customs Attaché, American Embassy, D. Building, 58 Rue La Boetie, Room 211, 75008 Paris, France, 265-7400, Ext. 8241.

Germany
Customs Attaché, American Embassy, Room 2069, 5300 Mehlemer Aue, Bonn-Bad Godesberg, Germany, 89-3207.

Hong Kong
Senior Customs Representative, American Consulate General, 26 Garden Road, Hong Kong, British Crown Colony, phone 5-239-011, Ext. 243.

Italy
Customs Attaché, American Embassy, Via Veneto 119, Room 302, 00187 Rome, Italy, phone 4674, Ext. 475.

Japan
Customs Attaché, American Embassy, Room 202, Akasaka I-chome, Minato-Ku, Tokyo 107, Japan, phone 583-7141, Ext. 7205.

Mexico
Customs Attaché, American Embassy, Paseo de la Reforma 305, Colonia Cuahtemoc, Mexico, D.F., phone 553-3333.

Taiwan
Customs Attaché, 2 Chun Hsiao West Rod., Second Section, Taipei, Taiwan, phone 333-551, Ext. 224.

APPENDIX A

STATE CONTACTS FOR EXPORT

Alabama

Alabama Development Office
  State Capitol
Montgomery, AL 36130
(205)263-0048

Alabama State Docks
P.O. Box 1588
Mobile, AL 36633
(205)690-6113

Alabama World Trade Association
P.O. Box 1508
Mobile, AL 36633

Center for International Trade
  & Commerce
Suite 131, 250 N. Water St.
Mobile, AL 36633
(205)433-1151

Governor's Office of International
  Trade
P.O. Box 2939
Montgomery, AL 36105-0930
(205)284-8722

International Trade Center,
  University of Alabama
P.O. Box 6186
University, AL 35486
(205)348-7621

North Alabama International
  Trade Association
P.O. Box 927
Huntsville, AL 35804
(205)532-3570

Alaska

Alaska Department of Commerce
and Economic Development
Pouch D
Juneau, AK 99811
(907)465-2500

Alaska State Chamber of
Commerce
310 Second St.
Juneau, AK 99801
(907)586-2323

Anchorage Chamber of Commerce
415 F St.
Anchorage, AK 99501
(907)272-2401

Fairbanks Chamber of Commerce
First National Center
100 Cushman St.
Fairbanks, AK 99707
(907)452-1105

Arizona

American Graduate School
of International Management
Thunderbird Campus
Glendale, AZ 85306
(602)978-7115

Arizona District Export Council
Box 26685
Tucson, AZ 85726
(602)748-7555

Arizona-Mexico Commission
P.O. Box 13564
Phoenix, AZ 85002
(602)255-1345

Arizona Office of Economic
Planning and Development
1700 W. Washington, 4th Floor
Phoenix, AZ 85007
(602)255-5371

Arizona World Trade Association
c/o Phoenix Chamber of Commerce
34 W. Monroe, Suite 900
Phoenix, AZ 85003
(602)254-5521

Consular Corps of Arizona
8331 E. Rose Lane
Scottsdale, AZ 85253
(602)947-6011

Sunbelt World Trade Association
7119 Sabino Vista Circle
Tucson, AZ 85715
(602)866-0364

Arkansas

Arkansas Association of Planning
and Development Districts
Federal Building
Little Rock, AR 72201
(501)378-5637

Arkansas Exporters Round Table
1660 Union National Plaza
Little Rock, AR 72201
(501)375-5377

Arkansas Industrial Development
Commission
One State Capital Mall
Little Rock, AR 72201
(501)371-7678

District Export Council
Savers Bldg., Suite 635
Capital at Spring St.
Little Rock, AR 72201
(501)378-5794

International Trade Center
University of Arkansas at
Little Rock
33rd and University
Little Rock, AR 72204
(501)371-2992

World Trade Club of
 Northeast Arkansas
P.O. Box 2566
Jonesboro, AR 72401
(501)932-7550

California

California Association of Port
 Authorities
1510 14th St.
Sacramento, CA 95816
(916)446-6339

California Chamber of Commerce
1027 10th St.
P.O. Box 1736
Sacramento, CA 95808
(916)444-6670

California Council for
 International Trade
77 Jack London Sq., Suite L
Oakland, CA 94607
(415)452-0770

California Department of Commerce
Office of Business Development
1121 L St., Suite 600
Sacramento, CA 95814

California State World Trade
 Commission
1121 L. St., Suite 310
Sacramento, CA 95814
(916)324-5511

Custom Brokers and Freight
 Forwarders Association
303 World Trade Center
San Francisco, CA 94111
(415)982-7788

Economic Development
 Corporation of Los Angeles County
1052 W. 6th St., Suite 510
Los Angeles, CA 90017
(213)482-5222

Export Managers Assn. of California
10919 Vanowen St.
North Hollywood, CA 91605
(818)985-1158

Foreign Trade Assn. of South
 California
350 S. Figueroa St., Rm. 226
Los Angeles, CA 90071
(213)627-0634

Inland International Trade Assn.
World Trade Center
W. Sacramento, CA 95691
(916)371-8000

International Business Assn., Long
 Beach Area Chamber of Commerce
100 Oceangate Plaza, Suite 50
Long Beach, CA 90802

International Business Council
Century City Chamber of Commerce
2020 Ave. of the Stars, Plaza Level
Century City, CA 90067
(213)553-4062

International Managers' Assn.
 of San Francisco
Custom House, P.O. Box 2425
San Francisco, CA 94126
(415)981-6690

International Marketing Assn. of
 Orange County
Irene Lange
California State—Fullerton,
 Marketing Department
Fullerton, CA 92634
(714)773-2223

Los Angeles Area Chamber of
 Commerce
International Commerce
404 S. Bixel St.
Los Angeles, CA 90017
(213)629-0722

North California District
  Export Council
450 Golden Gate Ave.
Box 36013
San Francisco, CA 94102
(415)556-5868

Oakland World Trade Assn.
1939 Harrison St.
Oakland, CA 94612
(415)388-8829

San Diego Chamber of Commerce
110 West C St., Suite 1600
San Diego, CA 92101
(619)232-0124

San Diego District Export Council
P.O. Box 81404
San Diego, CA 92138
(619)293-5395

San Francisco International
  Trade Council
P.O. Box 6052
San Francisco, CA 94101
(415)332-9100

San Francisco World Trade Assn.
San Francisco Chamber of Commerce
465 California St., 9th Floor
San Francisco, CA 94104
(415)392-4511

Santa Clara Valley World Trade Assn.
P.O. Box 6178
San Jose, CA 95150
(408)998-7000

South California District Export
  Council
11777 San Vicente Blvd.
Los Angeles, CA 90049
(213)209-6707

Valley International Trade Assn.
(San Fernando Valley)
c/o QUEP Secretarial Service
21133 Victory Blvd., Suite 221
Canoga Park, CA 91303
(818)704-8626

World Trade Assn. of Orange County
200 E. Sandpoint Ave., Suite 480
Santa Ana, CA 92707
(714)549-4160

World Trade Center Assn. of
  San Diego
P.O. Box 81404
San Diego, CA 92138
(619)298-6581

World Trade Council of
  San Mateo County
4 West 4th Ave., Suite 501
San Mateo, CA 94402
(415)342-7278

Colorado

Affiliated Advertising Agencies
  International World
  Headquarters
1393 East Iliff Ave.
Aurora, CO 80014
(303)750-1231

Colorado Assn. of Commerce
  and Industry
1390 Logan St.
Denver, CO 80202
(303)831-7411

Colorado Division of Commerce
  and Development
1313 Sherman St., Rm. 523
Denver, CO 80203
(303)866-2205

Denver Chamber of Commerce
1301 Welton St.
Denver CO 80204
(303)535-3211

International Trade Assn.
 of Colorado
Paul Bergman, Jr., President
c/o U.S. Department of Commerce
721 19th St., Rm. 113
Denver, CO 80202
(303)844-2900

Connecticut

Bridgeport Foreign Trade Zone
45 Lyon Terrace, Rm. 212
Bridgeport, CT 06604
(203)576-7221

Connecticut Department of
 Economic Development
210 Washington St.
Hartford, CT 06106
(203)566-3842

Connecticut District Export Council
450 Main St., Rm. 610B
Hartford, CT 06103
(203)722-3530

Connecticut Foreign Trade Assn.
c/o Manufacturing Assn. of
 South Connecticut
608 Ferry Blvd.
Stratford, CT 06497
(203)762-1000

Connecticut International Trade
 Assn.
c/o Suisman and Blumenthal
P.O. Box 119
Hartford, CT 06141

(Greater) Hartford Foreign
 Trade Zone
c/o Schuyler Corp.
999 Asylum Ave.
Hartford, CT 06105
(203)525-4451

(Greater) New Haven
 Chamber of Commerce
195 Church St.
New Haven, CT 06506
(203)787-6735

Quinnipiac College
Mt. Carmel Ave.
Hamden, CT 06518

Southwest Area Commerce
 and Industry Assn.
1 Landmark Sq., 2nd Floor
Stamford, CT 06901
(203)359-3220

West Connecticut International
 Trade Assn.
P.O. Box 787
Green Farms, CT 06436
(914)478-3131

Delaware

Delaware Development Office
P.O. Box 1401
Dover, DE 19903
(302)736-4271

Delaware-East Pennsylvania
 Export Council
9448 Federal Bldg.
600 Arch St.
Philadelphia, PA 19106
(215)597-2850

Delaware State Chamber of
  Commerce
One Commerce Center, Suite 200
Wilmington, DE 19801
(302)655-7221

Governor's International
  Trade Council
State of Delaware
Legislative Hall
Dover, DE 19901
(302)736-4136

Port of Wilmington
P.O. Box 1191
Wilmington, DE 19899
(302)571-4600

District of Columbia

American Enterprise Institute for
  Public Policy Research
1150 17th St., NW., Suite 1200
Washington, DC 20036
(202)862-58001

American National Metric Council
1010 Vermont Ave., NW.
Washington, DC 20005
(202)628-5757

American Management Assn.
440 1st St., NW.
Washington, DC 20001
(202)347-3092

American Society of International
  Law
2223 Massachusetts Ave., NW.
Washington, DC 20008
(202)265-4313

Bankers Assn. for Foreign Trade
1101 16th St., NW., Suite 501
Washington, DC 20036
(202)833-3060

Brookings Institution (The)
1775 Massachusetts Ave., NW.
Washington, DC 20036
(202)797-6000

Caribbean Central American Action
1333 New Hampshire Ave., NW.
Washington, DC 20036
(202)466-7464

Caribbean Council
2016 O St., NW.
Washington, DC 20036
(202)775-1136

Coalition for Employment
  Through Exports, Inc.
1801 K St., NW., 9th Floor
Washington, DC 20006
(202)296-6107

Committee for Economic
  Development
1700 K St., NW.
Washington, DC 20006
(202)296-5860

Emergency Committee for
  American Trade
1211 Connecticut Ave., Suite 801
Washington, DC 20036
(202)659-5147

Greater Washington Board of Trade
1129 20th St. NW.
Washington, DC 20036
(202)857-5900

Ibero American Chamber of
  Commerce
2100 M St., NW., Suite 607
Washington, DC 20037
(202)296-0335

State Contacts For Export 171

International Bank for
  Reconstruction & Development
1818 H St., NW.
Washington, DC 20006
(202)477-1234

International Economic Policy Assn.
1625 I St., NW.
Washington, DC 20006
(202)331-1974

International Finance Corp.
1818 H St., NW.
Washington, DC 20433
(202)477-1234

International Insurance Advisory
  Council
Chamber of Commerce of the
  United States
International Division
1615 H St., NW.
Washington, DC 20062
(202)463-5480

International Trade Council
750 13th St., SE.
Washington, DC 20003
(202)547-1727

Montgomery County Office of
  Economic Development
101 Monroe St., 15th Floor
Rockville, MD 20580
(301)251-2345

National Assn. of Manufacturers
1776 F St., NW.
Washington, DC 20006
(202)626-3700

National Assn. of State
Development Agency
Hall of State, Suite 345
444 North Capitol, NW.
Washington, DC 20001
(202)624-5411

National Council for U.S.
  China Trade
Suite 350
1050 17th St., NW.
Washington, DC 20036
(202)429-0340

National Industrial Council
1776 F St., NW.
Washington, DC 20006
(202)626-3853

Organization of American States
19th & Constitution Ave., NW.
Washington, DC 20006
(202)789-3000

Overseas Development Council
1717 Massachusetts Ave., NW.
Suite 501
Washington, DC 20036
(202)234-8701

Pan American Development Fund
1889 F St., NW.
Washington, DC 20006
(202)789-3969

Partners of the Americas
1424 K St., NW.
Washington, DC 20006
(202)628-3300

Partnership for Productivity
  International
2441 18th St. NW.
Washington, DC 20009
(202)234-0340

Trade Relations Council of the
  United States, Inc.
1001 Connecticut Ave., NW.
Room 901
Washington, DC 20036
(202)785-4194

172   Appendix A

The U.S.-Yugoslav Economic
 Council, Inc.
1511 K St., NW., Suite 431
Washington, DC 20005
(202)737-9652

Washington Agribusiness
 Promotion Council
14th & Independence Ave.,
 Room 3120
Auditors Building
Washington, DC 20250
(202)382-8006

Florida

Florida Council of International
 Development
2701 Le Jeune Rd., Suite 330
Coral Gables, FL 33134
(305)448-4035

Florida Customs Brokers and
 Forwarders Assn.
P.O. Box 522022
Miami Springs, FL 33166
(305)871-7177

Florida Department of Commerce
Bureau of International Trade
Collins Bldg.
107 W. Gaines St.
Tallahassee, FL 32304
(904)488-6124

Florida Department of Commerce
Caribbean Basin Development Center
2701 LeJeune Rd., Suite 330
Coral Gables, FL 33134
(305)446-8106

Florida Department of Commerce
2701 LeJeune Rd., Suite 330
Coral Gables, FL 33134
(305)446-8106

Florida District Export Council
c/o Miami Commerce District Office
Fed. Bldg., Suite 224
51 SW. 1st Ave.
Miami, FL 33140
(305)350-5267

Florida Exporters and Importers
 Assn.
P.O. Box 450648
Miami, FL 33145
(305)446-6646

Florida International Bankers Assn.
800 Douglas Entrance, Suite 21
Coral Gables, FL 33134
(305)446-6646

Florida Small Business
 Development Center
University of Florida
P.O. Box 32026
Pensacola, FL 32514

Fort Lauderdale Area World
 Trade Council
208 SE. 3rd Ave.
Ft. Lauderdale, FL 33302

International Center of Florida
800 Douglas Entrance, Suite 211
Coral Gables, FL 33134
(305)446-6646

Jacksonville International
 Trade Assn.
P.O. Box 329
Jacksonville, FL 32201
(904)353-0300

(City of) Miami
Bureau of International Trade
174 E. Flagler St., 7th Floor
Miami, FL 33133
(305)579-3324

Okaloosa/Walton County
  Area World Trade Council
P.O. Drawer 640
Fort Walton Beach, FL 32548
(904)224-5151

Orlando World Trade Assn.
75 E. Ivanhoe Blvd.
Orlando, FL 32804
(305)425-1234

Pensacola World Trade Council
40 N. Palasox St., Suite 400
Pensacola, FL 32501
(904)438-4081

Space Coast World Trade Council
1005 E. Strawbridge Ln.
Melbourne, FL 32901
(305)724-5400

Sun Coast Export Council
St. Petersburg Area Chamber
  of Commerce
P.O. Box 1371
St. Petersburg, FL 33731
(813)821-4069

Tampa Bay International
  Trade Council
P.O. Box 420
Tampa, FL 33601
(813)228-7777

World Trade Council, Palm
  Beach County
1983 PGA Blvd.
N. Palm Beach, FL 33408
(305)832-5955

World Trade Council, Bolusia County
P.O. Box 5702
Daytona Beach, FL 32018
(904)255-8131

Georgia

Georgia Department of
  Agriculture
328 Agriculture Bldg.
Atlanta, GA 30334
(404)656-3740

Georgia Ports Authority
P.O. Box 2406
Savannah, GA 31412
(912)964-1721

Georgia Department of
  Industry & Trade
1400 N. Omni International
P.O. Box 1776
Atlanta, GA 30301
(404)656-3571

Business Council of Georgia
575 N. Omni International
Atlanta, GA 30335
(404)223-2263

Hawaii

Chamber of Commerce of
  Hawaii/World Trade Assn.
735 Bishop St.
Honolulu, HI 96813
(808)531-4111

Hawaii Department of Planning
  and Ecomonic Development
International Services Branch
P.O. Box 2359
Honolulu, HI 96806
(808)548-3048

Economic Development Corp.
  of Honolulu
1001 Bishop St.
Pacific Tower, Suite 855
Honolulu, HI 96813
(808)545-4533

Idaho

Division of Economic &
  Community Affairs
Statehouse, Rm. 108
Boise, ID 83720
(208)334-3417

International Trade Committee
Greater Boise Chamber of Commerce
P.O. Box 2368
Boise, ID 82701
(208)344-5515

Idaho World Trade Association
Box 660
Twin Falls, ID 83301
(208)326-5116

District Export Council
Statehouse, Rm. 225
Boise, ID 83720
(208)334-2200

Idaho International Institute
1112 S. Owyhee
Boise, ID 83705

Illinois

American Assn. of Exporters &
  Importers
7763 S. Kedzie Ave.
Chicago, IL 60652
(312)471-1958

Automotive Exporters Club of
  Chicago
3205 S. Shields Ave.
Chicago, IL 60616
(312)567-6500
Toll Free (800)621-1552

Carnets
U.S. Council for International
  Business
1900 E. Golf Rd., Suite 740
Schaumburg, IL 60195
(708)490-9696

Central Illinois Coordinating
  Committee for International
  Trade
205 Arcade Bldg.
725 Wright St.
Champaign IL 61820
(217)333-1465

Chamber of Commerce of
  Upper Rock Island County
622 19th St.
Moline, IL 61265
(309)762-3661

Chicago Assn. of Commerce
  & Industry
World Trade Division
200 N. Lasalle
Chicago, IL 60603
(312)580-6900

Chicago Convention & Tourism
  Bureau
McCormick Place-on-the-Lake
Chicago, IL 60616
(312)225-5000

Chicago Economic Development
  Commission
International Business Division
20 N. Clark St., 28th Floor
Chicago, IL 60602
(312)744-8666

Chicago Midwest Credit
  Management Assn.
315 South NW. Hwy.
Park Ridge, IL 60068
(708)696-3000

State Contacts For Export 175

Chicago Regional Port District
12800 S. Butler at Lake Calumet
Chicago, IL 60633
(312)646-4400

Customs Brokers & Foreign
 Freight Forwarders Assn. of
 Chicago
P.O. Box 66365
Chicago, IL 60666
(312)992-4100

Foreign Credit Insurance Assn.
20 N. Clark St., Suite 910
Chicago, IL 60602
(312)641-1915

Illinois Department of Agriculture
1010 Jorie Blvd.
Oak Brook, IL 60521
(708)920-9256

Illinois Department of Commerce
 & Community Affairs
International Business Division
100 W. Randolph St.
Chicago, IL 60601
(312)814-7164

Illinois District Export Council
55 E. Monroe, RM. 1406
Chicago, IL 60603
(312)353-4450

Illinois Manufacturers' Assn.
175 W. Jackson Blvd., Suite 1321
Chicago, IL 60604
(312)922-6575

International Business Council
 MidAmerica (IBCM)
401 N. Wabash Ave., Suite 538
Chicago, IL 60611
(312)222-1424

Mid-America International
 Agri-Trade Council
828 Davis St.
Evanston, IL 60201
(708)368-4448

Northwest International
 Trade Club
P.O. Box 454
Elk Grove Village, IL 60007
(708)793-2086

Overseas Sales and Marketing Assn.
 of America
3500 Devon Ave.
Lake Bluff, IL 60044
(708)679-6070

Peoria Area Chamber of Commerce
230 SW. Adams St.
Peoria, IL 61602
(309)676-0755

The U.S.A.-Republic of China
 Economic Council
200 Main St.
Crystal Lake, IL 60014
(815)459-5875

U.S. Customs Service
55 E. Monroe, Suite 1501
Chicago, IL 60603
(312)686-2143

U.S. Great Lakes Shipping Assn.
3434 E. 95th St.
Chicago, IL 60617
(312)978-0342

World Trade Club of Northern
 Illinois
515 N. Court
Rockford, IL 61101
(815)987-8100

Indiana

Forum for International
  Professional Services
One Merchants Plaza, Suite 770S
Indianapolis, IN 46255
(317)267-7309

Hudson Institute
620 Union Dr.
P.O. Box 648
Indianapolis, IN 46206
(317)632-1787

International Banking Committee
Indiana Bankers Assn.
1 N. Capitol, Suite 315
Indianapolis, IN 46204
(317)632-9533

International Center of
  Indianapolis
1050 W. 42nd St.
Indianapolis, IN 46208
(317)923-1468

International Development Group
Fort Wayne Chamber of Commerce
826 Ewing St.
Fort Wayne, IN 46802
(219)424-1435

International Law Section
Indiana State Bar Assn.
230 E. Ohio St.
Indianapolis, IN 46204
(317)639-5465

Indiana Assn. of Credit
  Management
International Credit Management
130 E. New York St.
Indianapolis, IN 46204
(317)632-4444

Indiana Consortium for
  International Programs
N. Quad 240
Ball State University
Muncie, IN 47306
(317)285-8780

Indiana Council on World Affairs
Institute of Transnational Business
Ball state University
Muncie, IN 47306
(317)285-5526

Indiana Department of Commerce
Agriculture Division
One N. Capitol, Suite 700
Indianapolis IN 46204
(317)232-8770

Indiana Department of Commerce
International Trade Division
Indiana Commerce Center, Suite 700
One N. Capitol
Indianapolis, IN 46204-2243
(317)232-8845

Indiana Export Council
c/o U.S. Department of Commerce
Suite 700
1 N. Capitol
Indianapolis, IN 46204
(317)269-6214

Indiana Manufacturers Assn.
15 N. Pennsylvania St., Rm. 950
Indianapolis, IN 46204
(317)632-2474

Indiana Port Commission
  Headquarters
143 W. Market St., Suite 204
Indianapolis, IN 46204
(317)232-7150

State Contacts For Export

Indiana State Chamber of Commerce
1 North Capitol, Suite 200
Indianapolis, IN 46204
(317)634-6407

Indianapolis Airport Authority
Indianapolis International Airport
P.O. Box 51605
Indianapolis, IN 46241
(317)248-9594

Indianapolis Business
   Development Foundation
One Virginia Ave., 2nd Floor
Indianapolis, IN 46204
(317)639-6131

Indianapolis Chamber of Commerce
310 N. Meridian
Indianapolis, IN 46204
(317)267-2900

Indianapolis Economic
   Development Corporation
48 Monument Circle
Indianapolis, IN 46204
(317)236-6262

Indianapolis Foreign Trade Zone
   Park Fletcher Industrial
   Research Center
5545 W. Minnesota St.
P.O. Box 51681
Indianapolis, IN 46251
(317)247-1181

Michiana World Trade Club
401 E. Colfax, Suite 310
P.O. Box 1677
South Bend, IN 46634
(219)234-0051

Southwind-Maritime Center
P.O. Box 529
Mount Vernon, IN 47620
(812)838-4382

Tippecanoe World Trade Council
Greater Lafayette Chamber of
   Commerce
P.O. Box 348
Lafayette, IN 47902
(317)742-4041

Tri-State World Trade Council
329 Main St.
Evansville, IN 47708
(812) 425-8147

U.S. Customs Service
Indianapolis Airport
P.O. Box 51612
Indianapolis, IN 46251-0612
(317)248-4060

World Trade Club of Indiana
P.O. Box 986
Indianapolis, IN 46206
(317)285-5207

Iowa

International Trade Bureau
P.O. Box 4860
Cedar Rapids, IA 52407
(319)398-5310

Iowa Assn. of Business & Industry
706 Employers Mutual Bldg.
Des Moines, IA 50309
(505)281-3138

Iowa Development Commission
600 E. Court Ave., Suite A
Des Moines, IA 50309
(515)281-3581

Iowa-Illinois International Trade
   Assn.
112 E. 3rd St.
Davenport, IA 52801
(319)322-1706

Siouxland International Trade Assn.
Legislative and Agriculture Affairs
101 Pierce St.
Sioux City, IA 51101
(712)255-7903

Kansas

International Trade Institute
1627 Anderson
Manhattan, KS 66502
(913)532-7699

Kansas Board of Agriculture
109 SW. 9th St.
Topeka, KS 66612
(913)296-3736

Kansas-Northwest Missouri
  District Export Council
P.O. Box 626
Beloit, KS 67420
(913)738-2261

World Trade Council of Wichita
350 W. Douglas Ave.
Whichita, KS 67202
(316)265-7771

Kentucky

Bluegrass Area Development
  District
3220 Nicholasville Rd.
Lexington, KY 40503
(606)272-6656

Kentucky Commerce Cabinet
Office of International Marketing
Capital Plaza Tower, 24th Floor
Frankfort, KY 40601
(502)564-2170

Kentucky District Export Council
P.O. Box 33247
Louisville, KY 40232
(502)966-0550

Kentuckiana World Commerce
  Council
P.O. Box 58456
Louisville, KY 40258
(502)583-5551

(City of) Louisville
609 W. Jefferson St.
Louisville, KY 40202
(502)587-3051

North Kentucky Chamber of
  Commerce
1717 Dixie Hwy.
Covington, KY 41011
(606)341-9500

TASKIT (Technical Assistance
  to Stimulating Kentucky
  International Trade)
College of Business and Economics
University of Kentucky
Lexington, KY 40506-0205
(606)257-7663

Louisiana

Chamber of Commerce/
  New Orleans and River Region
301 Camp St.
New Orleans, LA 70130
(504)527-6900

International Trade Mart
Executive Offices, Suite 2900
2 Canal St.
New Orleans, LA 70130
(504)529-1601

Louisiana Department of Commerce
Office of International Trade,
  Finance and Development
P.O. Box 94185
Baton Rouge, LA 70804-9185
(504)342-5362

State Contacts For Export

Port of New Orleans
P.O. Box 60046
New Orleans, LA 701060
(504)528-3259

World Trade Club of Greater
  New Orleans
1132 International Trade Mart
2 Canal St.
New Orleans, LA 70130
(504)525-7201

Maine

Maine State Development Office
State House, Station 59
Augusta, ME 04333
(207)289-2656

Maine World Trade Assn.
1 Memorial Circle
Augusta, ME 04330
(207)622-0234

Maryland

Greater Baltimore Committee
2 Hopkins Plaza, Suite 900
Baltimore, MD 21201
(301)727-2820

Baltimore Economic Development
  Corp.
36 S. Charles St., Suite 2400
Baltimore, MD 21201
(301)837-9305

(The) Export Club
326 N. Charles St.
Baltimore, MD 21201
(301)837-9305

Maryland Department of Economic
  & Community Development
45 Calvert St.
Annapolis, MD 21401
(301)269-3176

Maryland/Washington, D.C.,
  Export Council
415 U.S. Customhouse
Gay and Lombard Sts.
Baltimore, MD 21202
(301)962-3560

Massachusetts

Associated Industries of
  Massachusetts
462 Boylston St.
Boston, MA 02116
(617)262-1180

Central Berkshire Chamber
  of Commerce
Berkshire Common
Pittsfield, MA 01201
(413)499-4000

Chamber of Commerce of
  Attleboro Area
42 Union St.
Attleboro, MA 02703
(617)222-0801

Commonwealth of Massachusetts
1 Ashburton Pl.
Boston, MA 02108
(617)727-8380

Fall River Area Chamber of
  Commerce
200 Pocasset St.
P.O. Box 1871
Fall River, MA 02722
(617)676-8226

Appendix A

Foreign Trade Zone No. 28
Industrial Development
  Commission
1213 High St.
Boston, MA 02110
(617)997-6501

Greater Boston Chamber of
  Commerce
125 High St.
Boston, MA 02110
(617)426-1250

Greater Lawrence Chamber of
  Commerce
300 Essex St.
Lawrence, MA 01840
(617)687-9404

Greater Springfield Chamber of
  Commerce
600 Bay State W. Plaza, Suite 600
1500 Main St.
Springfield, MA 01115
(413)734-5671

International Business Center
  of New England
22 Batterymarch St.
Boston, MA 02109
(617)542-0426

Massachusetts Commission
  on International Trade &
  Foreign Investment
State House, Suite 413F
Boston, MA 02133
(617)722-1673

Massachusetts Department of
  Commerce & Development
100 Cambridge St.
Boston, MA 02202
(517)727-3218

Massachusetts Department of
  Food & Agriculture
100 Cambridge St.
Boston, MA 02202
(617)727-3108

Massport
99 High St.
Boston, MA 02110
(617)482-2930

National Marine Fisheries Service
14 Elm St.
Gloucester, MA 01930
(617)281-3600

New Bedford Area Chamber
  of Commerce
First National Bank Bldg., Rm. 407
New Bedford, MA 02742
(617)999-5231

New England Governors'
  Conference
76 Summer St.
Boston, MA 02110
(617)423-6900

North Suburban Chamber of
  Commerce
25-B Montvale Ave.
Woburn, MA 01801
(617)933-3499

Smaller Business Assn. of
  New England
69 Hickory Drive
Waltham, MA 02154
(617)890-9070

South Middlesex Area
  Chamber of Commerce
615 Concord St.
Framingham, MA 01701
(617)879-5600

State Contacts For Export

South Shore Chamber of Commerce
36 Miller Stile Rd.
Quincy, MA 02169
(617)479-1111

Waltham/West Suburban
  Chamber of Commerce
663 Main St.
Waltham, MA 02154
(617)894-4700

Watertown Chamber of Commerce
75 Main St.
Watertown, MA 02172
(617)926-1017

Worcester Chamber of Commerce
Mechanics Tower, Suite 350
100 Front St.
Worcester, MA 01608
(617)753-2924

Michigan

Adcraft Club of Detroit
2630 Book Bldg.
Detroit, MI 48226
(313)962-7225

Ann Arbor Chamber of Commerce
207 E. Washington
Ann Arbor, MI 48104
(313)665-4433

BC/CAL/KAL/Port of Battle Creek
Foreign Trade Zone No. 43
P.O. Box 1438
Battle Creek, MI 49016
(616)968-8197

City of Detroit
Community & Economic
  Development Department
150 Michigan Ave. 7th Floor
Detroit, MI 48226
(313)224-6533

Detroit Customhouse Brokers and
  Foreign Freight Forwarders Assn.
155 W. Congress, Rm. 420
Detroit, MI 48226
(313)962-4681

Detroit/Wayne County Port
  Authority
100 Renaissance Center,
Suite 1370
Detroit, MI 48243
(313)259-8077

Downriver Community Conference
15100 Northline
Southgate, MI 48195
(313)283-8933

Flint Area Chamber of Commerce
708 Root, Rm. 123
Fling, MI 48503
(313)232-7101

Greater Port Huron-Marysville
  Chamber of Commerce
920 Pine Grove Ave.
Port Huron, MI 48060
(313)985-7101

Greater Saginaw Chamber of
  Commerce
901 S. Washington
Saginaw, MI 48606
(517)752-7161

Great Lakes Trade Adjustment
  Assistance Center
Institute of Science & Technology
University of Michigan
2901 Baxter Rd.
Ann Arbor, MI 48109
(313)763-4085

Greater Detroit Chamber of
  Commerce
150 Michigan Ave.
Detroit, MI 48226
(313)964-4000

Appendix A

Greater Grand Rapids Chamber of Commerce
17 Fountain St., NW.
Grand Raids, MI 49502
(616)459-7221

Kalamazoo Chamber of Commerce
P.O. Box 1169
Kalamazoo, MI 49007
(616)381-4000

Macomb County Chamber of Commerce
10 North Ave.
Mt. Clemens, MI 48043

Michigan Bankers Assn.
6105 W. St. Joseph Hwy.
Lansing, MI 48917
(517)321-1600

Michigan Department of Agriculture
P.O. Box 30017
Lansing, MI 48909
(517)373-1054

Michigan Department of Commerce
Office of International Development
P.O. Box 30105
Lansing, MI 48909
(517)373-6390

Michigan District Export Council
445 Fed. Bldg.
Detroit, MI 48226
(313)226-3650

Michigan Manufacturers Assn.
124 E. Kalamazoo
Lansing, MI 48933
(517)372-5900

Michigan State Chamber of Commerce
Small Business Programs
200 N. Washington Sq., Suite 400
Lansing, MI 48933
(517)371-2100

Motor Vehicle Manufacturers Assn. of USA
300 New Center Bldg.
Detroit, MI 48202
(313)872-4311

Muskegon Area Chamber of Commerce
1065 4th St.
Muskegon, MI 49441
(616)722-3751

Technology International Council
207 E. Washington St.
Ann Arbor, MI 48104
(313)665-4433

Twin Cities Area Chamber of Commerce
P.O. Box 1208
685 W. Main St.
Benton Harbor, MI 49022
(616)925-0044

U.S. Customs Service
Patrick V. McNamara Building
2nd Floor
Detroit, MI 48226
(313)226-3177

West Michigan World Trade Club
P.O. Box 2242
Grand Rapids, MI 49501
(616)456-9622

World Trade Club of Detroit
150 Michigan Ave.
Detroit, MI 48226
(313)964-4000

Minnesota

Minnesota Export Finance
 Authority
90 W. Plato Blvd.
St. Paul, MN 55107
(612)297-4659

Minnesota Trade Office
90 W. Plato Blvd.
St. Paul, MN 55107
(612)297-4655

Minnesota World Trade Assn.
33 E. Wentworth Ave., 101
West St. Paul, MN 55118
(612)457-1038

Minnesota World Trade Center
1300 Conwed Tower
444 Cedar St.
St. Paul, MN 55101
(612)297-1580

Seaway Port Authority of Duluth
P.O. Box 6877
Duluth, MN 55806
(218)727-8525

Mississippi

Greenville Port Commission
P.O. Box 446
Greenville, MS 38701
(601)335-2683

International Trade Club of
 Mississippi
P.O. Box 16353
Jackson, MS 39236
(601)956-1715

Jackson County Port Authority
P.O. Box 70
Pascagoula, MS 39567
(601)762-4041

Mississippi Department of
 Economic Development
Marketing Division
P.O. Box 849
Jackson, MS 39205
(601)359-3444

Mississippi State Port Authority
 at Gulfport
P.O. Box 40
Gulfport, MS 39502
(601)865-4306

Missouri

International Trade Club of
 Greater Kansas City
920 Main St., Suite 600
Kansas City, MO 64105
(816)221-1460

Greater Ozarks International
 Trade Club
P.O. Box 1687
Springfield, MO 65805
(417)862-5567

Missouri Department of
 Agriculture
International Marketing Division
P.O. Box 630
Jefferson, City, MO 65102
(314)751-5611

Missouri Department of Commerce
International Business Office
P.O. Box 118
Jefferson City, MO 65102
(314)751-4855

Missouri District Export Council
120 S. Central, Suite 400
St. Louis, MO 63105
(314)425-3302

World Trade Club of St. Louis
111 N. Taylor Ave.
Kirkwood, MO 63122
(314)965-9940

Montana

49th Parallel Institute
Department of Political Science
Montana State University
Bozeman, MT 59717
(406)994-6690

Montana Department of Commerce
Business Assistance Division
1424 9th Ave.
Helena, MT 59620
(406)444-3923

Nebraska

Midwest International Trade Assn.
c/o NBC, 13th & O Sts.
Lincoln, NE 68108
(402)472-4321

Nebraska Department of Economic
   Development State Development &
   International Division
301 Centennial Mall S.
Lincoln, NE 68509
(402)471-4670

Omaha Chamber of Commerce
1301 Harney St.
Omaha, NE 68102
(402)346-5000

Nevada

Commission on Economic
   Development
600 E. Williams, Suite 203
Carson City, NV 89710
(702)885-4325

Economic Development
   Authority of West Nevada
P.O. Box 11710
Reno, NV 89510
(702)322-4004

Latin Chamber of Commerce
P.O. Box 7534
Las Vegas, NV 89125-2534
(702)385-7367

Nevada Development Authority
P.O. Box 11128
Las Vegas, NV 89111
(702)739-8222

Nevada District Export Council
P.O. Box 11007
Reno, NV 89520
(702)784-3401

New Hampshire

(State of) New Hampshire
Department of Resources and
   Economic Development
P.O. Box 856
Concord, NH 03301
(603)271-2341

South New Hampshire Assn.
   of Commerce & Industry
4 Manchester St.
P.O. Box 1123
Nashua, NH 03601
(603)882-8106

New Mexico

Economic Development &
   Tourist Department
International Division
Bataan Memorial Bldg.
Santa Fe, NM 87503
(505)827-3145

Foreign Trade Zone, New Mexico
P.O. Box 26928
Albuquerque, NM 87125
(505)842-0088

New Mexico Department of
  Agriculture
P.O. Box 5600
Las Cruces, NM 88003
(505)646-4929

New Mexico Foreign Trade &
  Investment Council
Mail Stop 150, Alvarado Sq.
Albuquerque, NM 87158
(505)848-4632

New Mexico Industry
  Development Corp.
300 San Mateo NE., Suite 815
Albuquerque, NM 87118

New Jersey

Delaware River Port Authority
World Trade Division
Bridge Plaza
Camden, NJ 08101
(609)963-6420, ext 264

International Business Council
240 W. State St., Suite 1412
Trenton, NJ 08608

International Round Table
Bergen County Community
  College
400 Paramus Rd.
Paramus, NJ 07652
(201)477-7167

(State of) New Jersey Division
  of International Trade
744 Broad St., Rm. 1709
Newark, NJ 07102
(201)648-3518

Rutgers Small Business
  Development Center
180 University Ave.
Newark, NJ (201)648-5950

Union County Chamber of Commerce
International Trade Committee
135 Jefferson Ave.
P.O. Box 300
Elizabeth, NJ 07207
(201)352-0900

U.S. Association of Credit and
  Finance Executives
Foreign Credit Division
P.O. Box 130
405 Washington Ave.
Kenilworth, NJ 07033
(201)272-9191

World Trade Assn. of New Jersey
5 Commerce St.
Newark, NJ 07102
(201)623-7070

New York

Albany-Colonie Regional
  Chamber of Commerce
14 Corporate Woods Blvd.
Albany, NY 12211
(518)434-1214

American Arbitration Assn.
140 West 51st St.
New York, NY 10020
(212)484-4000

American Assn. of Exporters and
  Importers
30th Floor, 11 West 42nd St.
New York, NY 10036
(212)944-2230

American Importers Assn.
11 West 42nd St.
New York, NY 10036
(212)944-2230

American Institute of Marine
  Underwriters
14 Wall St., 21st Floor
New York, NY 10005
(212)233-0550

Appendix A

American Management Associations
135 W. 50th St.
New York, NY 10020
(212)586-8100

Buffalo Area Chamber of Commerce
107 Delaware Ave.
Buffalo, NY 14202
(716)849-6682

Buffalo World Trade Assn.
538 Ellicott Sq. Bldg.
Buffalo, NY 14203
(716)854-1019

Conference Board (The)
845 Third Ave.
New York, NY 10022
(212)628-3200

Council on Foreign Relations, Inc.
58 East 68th St.
New York, NY 10021
(212)734-0400

Customs & International Trade
  Bar Assn.
c/o 40 Siegel Mandell and
  Davidson
1 Whitehall St.
New York, NY 10004
(212)425-0060

Foreign Credit Interchange
  Bureau—National Assoc. of
  Credit Managers
475 Park Ave. South
New York, NY 10016
(212)578-4410

Foreign Policy Assn.
205 Lexington Ave.
New York, NY 10016
(212)481-8450

Fund for Multi-National
  Mangement Education
680 Park Ave.
New York, NY 10021
(212)535-9386

International Advertising Assn.
475 Fifth Ave.
New York, NY 10077
(212)684-1583

International Airforwarders and
  Agents Assn.
Box 627
Rockville Center, NY 11571
(516)536-6229

International Business Council
  of Rochester Area
  Chamber of Commerce
International Trade and
  Transportation
55 St. Paul St.
Rochester, NY 14604
(716)454-2220

International Executives Assn.
114 East 32nd St.
New York, NY 10016
(212)683-9755

International Trade Council, Greater
  Syracuse Chamber of Commerce
100 E. Onondaga St.
Syracuse, NY 13202
(315)470-1343

International Executives Assn.
114 E. 32nd St., Suite 1301
New York, NY 10016
(212)683-9755

Long Island Assn.
80 Hauppage Rd.
Commack, NY 11725
(516)499-4400

State Contacts For Export

Mohawk Valley World Trade Council
P.O. Box 4126
Utica, NY 13540
(315)797-1630

National Assn. of Credit Managers
Foreign Credit Insurance Bureau
475 Park Ave. S.
New York, NY 10016
(212)578-4710

National Assn. of Credit
  Managers Upstate New York
250 Delaware Ave.
Buffalo, NY 14202
(716)845-7018

National Assn. of Export Companies
396 Broadway, Suite 603
New York, NY 10013
(212)966-2271

National Assn. of Export
  Management Companies
200 Madison Ave.
New York, NY 10016
(212)561-2025

National Committee on International
  Trade Documentation (The)
350 Broadway
New York, NY 10013
(212)925-1400

National Customs Brokers and
  Forwarders Assn. of America
One World Trade Center,
  Suite 1109
New York, NY 10048
(212)432-0050

National Export Traffic League
234 Fifth Ave.
New York, NY 10001
(212)697-5895

National Foreign Trade Council
11 West 42nd St., 30th Floor
New York, NY 10036
(212)944-2230

New York Chamber of Commerce
  & Industry
200 Madison Ave.
New York, NY 10016
(212)561-2028

New York State Department
  of Commerce
Division of International
  Commerce
230 Park Ave.
New York, NY 10169
(212)309-0500

Port Authority of New York and
  New Jersey Trade Development
  Office
Rm. 64-E
One World Trade Center
New York, NY 10048
(212)466-8333

Private Export Funding Corp.
280 Park Ave.
New York, NY 10017
(202)557-3100

Rochester Area Chamber of
  Commerce
World Trade Department
55 St. Paul St.
Rochester, NY 14604
(716)454-2220

Tappan Zee International
  Trade Assn.
One Blue Hill Plaza
Peal River, NY 10965
(914)735-7040

Appendix A

U.S. Council for International Business
1212 Ave. of the Americas
New York, NY 10036
(212)354-4480

The U.S.-U.S.S.R. Trade and Economic Council
805 3rd Ave., 14th Floor
New York, NY 10022
(202)644-4550

United States of America Business & Industry Advisory Committee
1212 Avenue of the Americas
New York, NY 10036
(212)354-4480

Westchester County Assn.
World Trade Club of Westchester
235 Mamaroneck Ave.
White Plains, NY 10605
(914)948-6444

World Commerce Assn. of Central New York
100 E. Onandago St.
Syracuse, NY 13202
(315)470-1343

World Trade Club of Long Island
c/o LIREX
1425 Old Country Road
Plainview, L.I., NY 11803

World Trade Club of New York
396 Broadway, Suite 603
New York, NY 10013
(212)966-2271

World Trade Institute
One World Trade Center
New York, NY 10048
(212)466-4044

North Carolina

North Carolina Department of Agriculture
P.O. Box 27647
Raleigh, NC 27611
(919)733-7912

North Carolina Department of Commerce
International Division
430 N. Salisbury St.
Raleigh, NC 27611
(919)733-7193

North Carolina State University
International Trade Center
P.O. Box 5125
Raleigh, NC 27650
(919)737-7912

North Carolina World Trade Assn.
P.O. Box 327
Wilmington, NC 28402
(919)763-9841

North Dakota

Fargo Chamber of Commerce
321 N. 4th St.
Fargo, ND 58108
(701)237-5678

North Dakota Economic Development Commission
Industrial Development
International Division
Liberty Memorial Bldg.
State Capital Grounds
Bismarck, ND 58505
(701)224-2810

Ohio

Academy of International Business
World Trade Education Center
Cleveland State University
Cleveland, OH 44115
(216)687-3733

State Contacts For Export

Cincinnati Council on World Affairs
1028 Dixie Terminal Bldg.
Cincinnati, OH 45202

Cleveland Council on World Affairs
601 Rockwell Ave.
Cleveland, OH 44114
(216)781-3730

Cleveland World Trade Assn.
690 Huntington Bldg.
Cleveland, OH 44115
(216)621-3300

Columbus Area Chamber of Commerce
37 N. High St.
Columbus, OH 43216
(614)221-1321

Columbus Council on World Affairs
57 Jefferson Ave.
Columbus, OH 43215
(614)461-0632

Commerce and Industry of Greater Elyria
P.O. Box 179
Elyria, OH 44036
(216)322-5438

Dayton Council on World Affairs
300 College Park
Dayton, OH 45469
(513)229-2319

Dayton Development Council
1980 Kettering Tower
Dayton, OH 45423-1980
(513)226-8222

Greater Cincinnati Chamber of Commerce
120 W. 5th St.
Cincinnati, OH 45202
(513)579-3143

Greater Cincinnati World Trade Assn.
120 W. 5th St.
Cincinnati, OH 45202
(513)579-3122

International Business & Trade Assn. of Akron
One Cascade Plaza, Suite 800
Akron, OH 44308
(216)379-3157

International Trade Institute
5055 N. Main St.
Dayton, OH 45415
(513)276-5995

North Central Ohio International Trade Club
Mansfield Richland Area Chamber of Commerce
55 N. Mulberry St.
Mansfield, OH 44902
(419)522-3211

North Ohio District Export Council
Plaza Nine Bldg.
55 Erieview Plaza, Suite 700
Cleveland, OH 44114
(216)522-4750

Ohio Department of Agriculture
Ohio Department Bldg., Rm. 607
65 S. Front St.
Columbus, OH 43215
(614)466-4104

Ohio Department of Development
International Trade Division
30 E. Broad St.
Columbus, OH 43216
(614)466-5017

Ohio Foreign Commerce Assn.
1111 Chester Ave., Rm. 506A
Cleveland, OH 44114
(216)696-7000
Port of Cleveland

Port of Cleveland
Cleveland-Cuyahoga County
  Port Authority
101 Erieside Ave.
Cleveland, OH 44114-1095
(216)241-8004

Port of Toledo
Toledo-Lucas County Port
  Authority
One Maritime Plaza
Toledo, OH 43604-1866
(419)243-8251

South Ohio District Export Council
9504 Fed. Bldg.
550 Main St.
Cincinnati, OH 45202
(513)684-2944

Toledo Area International Trade
  Assn.
218 Huron St.
Toledo, OH 43604
(419)243-8191

U.S. Customs Service
55 Erieview Plaza
Cleveland, OH 44114
(216)522-4284

World Trade Committee of
  Youngstown
Area Chamber of Commerce
200 Wick Bldg.
Youngstown, OH 44503-1474
(216)744-2131

World Trade Education Center
Cleveland State University
University Center Bldg.,
  Rm. 460
Cleveland, OH 44115
(216)687-3733

World Trade and Technology
  Center
10793 State Rte. 37 W.
Sunbury, OH 43074
(614)965-2974

Oklahoma

Foreign Trade Zone No. 53
Tulsa Port of Catoosa
5555 Bird Creek Ave.
Catoosa, OK 74015
(918)266-5830

Foreign Trade Zone No. 106
One Santa Fe Plaza
Oklahoma City, OK 73102
(405)278-8900

Metropolitan Tulsa Chamber
  of Commerce
Economic Development Division
616 S. Boston Ave.
Tulsa, OK 74119
(918)585-1201

Muskogee City-County Port
  Authority
Rte. 6, Port 50
Muskogee, OK 74401
(918)682-7886

Oklahoma City Chamber of
  Commerce
Economic and Community
  Development
One Santa Fe Plaza
Oklahoma City, OK 73102
(405)278-8900

Oklahoma City International
  Trade Assn.
P.O. Box 66
Perry, OK 73077
(405)336-4402

Oklahoma Department of
  Economic Development
International Division
4024 Lincoln Blvd.
Oklahoma, City, OK 73105
(405)521-2401

Oklahoma District Export Council
4024 Lincoln Blvd.
Oklahoma City, OK 73105
(405)231-5302

Oklahoma State Chamber of
  Commerce
4020 Lincoln Blvd.
Oklahoma City, OK 73105

Oklahoma State Department
  of Agriculture
2800 Lincoln Blvd.
Oklahoma City, OK 73105
(405)521-3864

Tulsa Port of Catoosa
5350 Cimarron Road
Catoosa, OK 74015
(918)266-2291

Tulsa World Trade Assn.
Burlington Northern Airfreight
1821 N. 106th E. Ave.
Tulsa, OK 74116
(918)836-0338

Oregon

Eugene Area Chamber of Commerce
1401 Willamette
P.O. Box 1107
Eugene, OR 97440
(503)484-1314

Institute for International Trade
  & Commerce
Portland State University
1912 S.W. Sixth Ave., Rm. 260
Portland, OR 97207
(503)229-3246

Oregon District Export Council
1220 SW. 3rd Ave., Rm. 618
Portland, OR 97209
(503)292-9219

Oregon Economic Development
  Department
Business Information Division
595 Cottage St., NE.
Salem, OR 97310
(503)373-1231

Pacific Northwest International
  Trade Assn.
200 SW. Market
Suite 220
Portland, OR 97201
(503)228-4361

Western Wood Products Assn.
Yeon Bldg.
Portland, OR 97204
(503)224-3930

Pennsylvania

American Society of International
  Executives
Dublin Hall, Suite 419
Blue Bell, PA 19422
(215)643-3040

Assessment of International
  Markets Program
382 Mervis Hall
University of Pittsburgh
Pittsburgh, PA 15260
(412)624-1777

Appendix A

Foreign Trade Zone No. 33
Regional Industrial Development
  Corp.
Union Trust Bldg.
Pittsburgh, PA 15219
(412)471-3939

International Business Forum
42 S. 15th St., Suite 315
Philadelphia, PA 19102
(215)822-6893

International Trade Executives
  Club of Erie
c/o Manufacturers Assn. of Erie
33 E. 8th St.
Erie, PA 16507
(814)459-3335

International Trade Executives
  Club of Pittsburgh
2002 Fed. Bldg.
1000 Liberty Ave.
Pittsburgh, PA 15222
(412)644-2850

North Central Pennsylvania
  Regional Planning and
  Development Commission
651 Montmorenci Ave.
Ridgeway, PA 15853
(814)773-3162

Northwest Pennsylvania Regional
  Planning and Development
  Commission
Biery Bldg., Suite 406
Franklin, PA 16323
(814)437-3024

Pennsylvania Department of
  Agriculture
Bureau of Agricultural
  Development
2301 N. Cameron St.
Harrisburg, PA 17110
(717)783-8460

Pennsylvania Department of
  Commerce
Bureau of Domestic &
  International Commerce
453 Forum Bldg.
Harrisburg, PA 17120
(717)787-7190

(City of) Philadelphia
Municipal Services Bldg.,
  Rm. 1660
Philadelphia, PA 19102
(215)686-3647

(Greater) Philadelphia
  Chamber of Commerce
1346 Chestnut St., Suite 800
Philadelphia, PA 19107
(215) 545-1234

Philadelphia Export Network
3508 Market St., Suite 100
Philadelphia, PA 19104
(215)898-4189

Philadelphia Port Corporation
6th & Chestnut St.
Philadelphia, PA 19106
(215)928-9100

Pittsburgh Consular Association
Consul de Mexico, Suite 3201
4297 Greensburg Pike
Pittsburgh, PA 15221
(412)271-5900

Pittsburgh Council for
  International Visitors
139 University Place
Pittsburgh, PA 15260
(412)624-7929

Port Authority of Allegheny
  County
514 Wood St.
Pittsburgh, PA 15222
(412) 237-7460

Port of Erie-West
507 Municipal Bldg.
Erie, PA 16501
(814)456-8561

Reading Foreign Trade Assn.
35 N. 6th St.
Reading, PA 19603
(215)320-2976

South Alleghenies Regional
  Planning & Development
  Commission
S. Alleghenies Plaza, Suite 100
1506 11th Ave.
Altoona, PA 16601
(814)946-1641

Southwest Pennsylvania
  Economic Development
  District
355 5th Ave., Rm. 141
Pittsburgh, PA 15222
(412)391-1240

Trade Adjustment Assistance
  Center
One E. Penn Sq., Suite 14
Philadelphia, PA 19107
(215)568-7740

Trade Adjustment Assistance
  Center
Investment Bldg., Rm. 1001
239 4th Ave.
Pittsburgh, PA 15222
(412)566-1732

U.S. Customs Service
822 Fed. Bldg.
1000 Liberty Ave.
Pittsburgh, PA 15222
(412)644-3589

West Pennsylvania District
  Export Council
1000 Liberty Ave., Rm. 2002
Pittsburgh, PA 15222
(412)644-2850

Women's International Trade Assn.
P.O. Box 40004, Continental
  Station
Philadelphia, PA 19106
(215)923-6900

World Trade Assn. of Philadelphia
820 Land Title Bldg.
Philadelphia, PA 19110
(215)563-8887

Puerto Rico

District Export Council
252 Tetuan St.
San Juan, P.R. 00901
(809)721-7600

Puerto Rico Chamber of Commerce
P.O. Box 3789
San Juan, P.R. 00904
(809)721-6060

Puerto Rico Department of
  Commerce
P.O. Box 4275
San Juan, P.R. 00905
(809)721-3290

Puerto Rico Economic
  Development Administration
GPO Box 2350
San Juan, P.R. 00936
(809)758-4747

Puerto Rico Manufacturers Assn.
P.O. Box 2410
Hato Rey, P.R. 00919
(809)759-9445

Puerto Rico Products Assn.
GPO Box 3631
San Juan, P.R. 00936
(809)753-8484

Rhode Island

(Greater) Providence Chamber
 of Commerce
10 Dorrance St.
Providence, RI 02903
(401)521-5000

Rhode Island Department of
 Economic Development
7 Jackson Walkway
Providence, RI 02903
(401)277-2601

South Carolina

Governor's Export Advisory
 Committee
Rt. 1, Box 501
Spartanburg, SC 29302
(803)579-3050

Low County International Trade Club
P.O. Box 159
Charleston, SC 29402
(803)571-0510

Midlands Trade Club
Rt. 2, Box 50A
Elgin, SC 29045
(803)254-1237

Pee Dee International Trade Club
P.O. Box 716
Kingstree, SC 29556
(803)382-9393

South Carolina State Development
 Board
P.O. Box 927
Columbia, SC 29202
(803)758-2384

South Carolina District
 Export Council
Strom Thurmond Federal Bldg.,
 Suite 172
1835 Assembly St.
Columbia, SC 29201
(803)765-5345

South Carolina State Port
 Authority
P.O. Box 817
Charleston, SC 29402
(803)577-8100

West South Carolina
 International Trade Club
P.O. Box 8764
Greenville, SC 29604-8764
(803)232-1045

South Dakota

Rapid City Area Chamber of
 Commerce
P.O. Box 747
Rapid City, SD 57709
(605)343-1744

Sioux Falls Chamber of Commerce
127 E. 10th St.
Sioux Falls, SD 57101
(605)336-1620

South Dakota Department of
 State Development
Capitol Lake Plaza
Pierre, SD 57501
(605)773-5032

Texas

Amarillo Chamber of Commerce
Amarillo Bldg.
301 S. Polk
Amarillo, TX 79101
(806)374-5238

State Contacts For Export

Brownsville Navigation District
 of Cameron County
P.O. Box 3070
Brownsville, TX 78520
(512)831-4592

Center for International Business
World Trade Center, Suite 184
P.O. Box 58428
Dallas, TX 75258
(214)742-7301

Dallas Chamber of Commerce
1507 Pacific
Dallas, 75201
(214)954-1111

Dallas Council on World Affairs
Fred Lange Center
1310 Annex, Suite 101
Dallas, TX 75204
(214)827-7960

El Paso Chamber of Commerce
10 Civic Center Plaza
El Paso, TX 79944
(915)544-7880

Foreign Credit Insurance Assn.
600 Travis, Suite 2860
Houston, TX 77002
(713)227-0987

Fort Worth Chamber of
 Commerce
700 Throckmorton
Fort Worth, TX 76102
(817)336-2491

Houston Chamber of Commerce
1100 Milan Bldg., 25th Floor
Houston, TX 77002
(713)651-1313

Houston District Export Council
6048 W. View Dr.
Houston, TX 77055
(713)686-4331

Houston Port Authority
1519 Capitol Ave., Box 2562
Houston, TX 77001
(713)225-0671

Houston World Trade Assn.
1520 Texas Ave., Suite 239
Houston, TX 77002
(713)225-0967

Lubbock Chamber of Commerce
14th St. & Ave. K
P.O. Box 561
Lubbock, TX 79408
(806)763-4666

North Dallas Chamber of Commerce
10707 Preston Road
Dallas, TX 75230
(214)368-6653

North Texas Commission
P.O. Box 61246
DFW Airport, TX 75261
(214)574-4430

North Texas Customs Brokers and
 Foreign Freight Forwarders Assn.
P.O. Box 225464
DFW Airport, TX 75261
(214)456-0730

North Texas District Export Council
448 Willow Lane
Dallas, TX 75234
(214)788-1340

Odessa Chamber of Commerce
P.O. Box 3626
Odessa, TX 79760
(915)332-9111

Port of Beaumont
P.O. Box Drawer 2297
Beaumont, TX 77704
(713)835-5367

Port of Corpus Christi
P.O. Box 1541
Corpus Christi, TX 78403
(512)882-5633

Port of Port Arthur
Box 1428
Port Arthur, TX 77640
(713)983-2011

(Greater) San Antonio
  Chamber of Commerce
P.O. Box 1628
San Antonio, TX 78296
(512)227-8181

Texas City Terminal Railway Co.
  (Port)
P.O. Box 591
Texas City, TX 77590
(713)945-4461

Texas Department of Agriculture
Export Services Division
P.O. Box 12847, Capitol Station
Austin, TX 78711
(512)475-2760

Texas Economic Development
  Commission
P.O. Box 12728, Capitol Station
Austin, TX 78711
(512)472-5039

Texas Foreign Trade Center of Dallas
P.O. Box 50007
Dallas, TX 75250
(214)570-1455

Texas Industrial Development
P.O. Box 1002
College Station, TX 77841
(409)845-2911

Texas International Business Assn.
P.O. Box 29334
Dallas, TX 75229
(214)692-1214

U.S. Chamber of Commerce
4835 LBJ Freeway, Suite 750
Dallas, TX 75324
(214)387-0404

U.S. Customs Service
P.O. Box 61050
DFW Airport, TX 75261
(214)574-2170

World Trade Assn. of
  Dallas/Fort Worth
P.O. Box 29334
Dallas, TX 75229
(214)760-9105

Tennessee

Chattanooga World Trade Council
1001 Market St.
Chattanooga, TN 37402

East Tennessee International
  Trade Club
P.O. Box 280
Knoxville, TN 37901
(615)971-2027

Memphis World Trade Club
P.O. Box 3577
Memphis, TN 38103
(901)320-2210

Mid-South Exporters Roundtable
P.O. Box 3521
Memphis, TN 38173
(901)320-5811

Middle Tennessee World
  Trade Club
1101 Kermit Dr., Suite 112
Nashville, TN 37217

Tennessee Department of
  Agriculture
Ellington Agricultural Center
P.O. Box 40627, Melrose Station
Nashville, TN 37204
(615)360-0103

Tennessee Department of Economic
  & Community Development
320 6th Ave., 7th Floor
Nashville, TN 37219-5308
(615)741-4815

Tennessee District Export Council
3074 Sidco Dr.
Nashville, TN 37210
(615)259-9300

Utah

Salt Lake Area Chamber of
  Commerce
Export Development Committee
19 E. 2nd St.
Salt Lake City, UT 84111

(State of) Utah
International Business
  Development Office
6150 State Office Bldg.
Salt Lake City, UT 84114
(801)533-5325

World Trade Assn. of Utah
2000 Beneficial Life Towers
Salt Lake City, UT 84111
(801)355-9333

Vermont

(Greater) Burlington Industrial
7 Burlington Sq.
P.O. Box 786
Burlington, VT 05402
(802)862-5726

(State of) Vermont Agency of
  Development & Community
  Affairs
Pavilion Office Bldg.
109 State St.
Montpelier, VT 05602

Virginia

Fairfax County Economic
  Development Authority
8330 Old Cournt House Rd.
Vienna, VT 22180
(703)790-0600

International Trade Association
  of North Virginia
P.O. Box 2982
Reston, VT 22090
(703)860-8795

Institute for International
  Development
354 Maple Ave. West
Vienna, VA 22108
(703)281-5040

Newport News Export Trading
  System
Department of Development
Peninsula Export Program
2400 Washington Ave.
Newport, News, VA 23607
(804)247-8751

Piedmont Foreign Trade Council
P.O. Box 1374
Lynchburg, VA 24505
(804)782-4231

VEXTRAC (Export Trading
  Company of Virginia
  Port Authority)
600 World Trade Center
Norfolk, VA 23510
(804)623-8000

Virginia Chamber of Commerce
611 E. Franklin St.
Richmond, VA 23219
(804)644-1607

Virginia Department of
 Agriculture & Consumer Affairs
1100 Bank St., Rm. 710
Richmond, VA 23219
(804)786-3501

Virginia Department of Economic
 Development
Washington Office Bldg., 9th Fl.
Richmond, VA 23219
(804)786-3791

Virginia District Export Council
P.O. Box 10190
Richmond, VA 23240
(804)771-2248

Washington

Economic Development
 Partnership of Puget Sound
18000 Pacific Hwy., Suite 400
Seattle, WA 98188
(206)433-1629

Export Assistance
Center of Washington
312 First Ave. N.
Seattle, WA 98109
(206)464-7123

Inland Empire World Trade Club
P.O. Box 3727
Spokane, WA 99220
(509)489-0500

National Marine Fisheries Service
Fisheries Development Division
7600 San Point Way NE.,
 Bin C15700
Seattle, WA 98115
(206)526-6117

Northwest Trade Adjustment
 Assistance Center
1900 Seattle Tower
1218 3rd Ave.
Seattle, WA 98101
(206)622-2730

Seattle Chamber of Commerce
Trade and Transportation
 Division
One Union Sq., 12th Floor
Seattle, WA 98101
(206)447-7263

Tri-Cities Chamber of Commerce
P.O. Box 2322
Kennewick, WA 99302
(509)735-1000

Washington Council of
 International Trade
4th and Vine Bldg., Suite 350
Seattle, WA 98121
(206)621-8485

Washington Public Ports Assn.
P.O. Box 1518
Olympia, WA 98507
(206)943-0760

Washington State Department
 of Commerce & Economic
 Development
International Trade and
 Investment Division
312 First Ave. N.
Seattle, WA 98109
(206)464-7149

Washington State International
 Trade Fair
999 3rd Ave.
3501 First Interstate Center
Seattle, WA 98104
(206)682-6900

State Contacts For Export

World Affairs Council
515 Madison Ave., Suite 526
Seattle, WA 98101
(206)621-0344

World Trade Club of Seattle
1402 3rd Ave., Suite 414
Seattle, WA 98104
(206)682-6900

World Affairs Council
515 Madison Ave., Suite 526
Seattle, WA 98104
(206)682-6986

World Trade Club of Seattle
1402 3rd Ave., Suite 414
Seattle, WA 98101
(206)621-0344

World Trade Committee of Bellevue
110 110th NE., Suite 300
Bellevue, WA 98004
(206)454-2464

West Virginia

West Virginia District Export Council
P.O. Box 26
Charleston, WV 25321
(304)343-8874

West Virginia Manufacturers Assn.
405 Capitol St., Suite 414
Charleston, WV 25301
(304)342-2123

West Virginia Department of
  Commerce
Economic Development
Rotunda 150, State Capitol
Charleston, WV 25305
(304)348-0400

West Virginia Chamber of Commerce
P.O. Box 2789
Charleston, WV 25330
(304)342-1115

Wisconsin

Foreign Trade Zone of
  Wisconsin Limited
2150 E. College Ave.
Cudahy, WI 53110
(414)764-2111

Milwaukee Assn. of Commerce
756 N. Milwaukee St.
Milwaukee, WI 53202
(414)273-3000

(Port of) Milwaukee
500 N. Harbor Dr.
Milwaukee, WI 53202
(414)278-3511

Small Business Development
  Center
602 State St.
Madison, WI 53703
(608)263-7766

Wisconsin Department of
  Development
123 W. Washington Ave.
Madison, WI 53707
(608)266-1767

Wyoming

State of Wyoming
Office of Governor
Herschler Bldg., 2nd Floor E.
Cheyenne, WY 82002
(307)777-7574

Other organizations also can help you to develop your contact list:

Argentina

American Embassy Commercial Section
4300 Columbia, 1425
Buenos Aires, Argentina
APO Miami 34034
Phone: 744-7611/8811/9911
Telex: 18156 USICA AR

American Chamber of Commerce in Argentina
Virrey Loreto 2477/81
1426 Buenos Aires, Argentina
Phone: 782-6016
Telex: 21517 CIARG AR

Embassy of Argentina Commercial Section
1667 K St., NW., Suite 610
Washington, DC 20006
Phone: (202)939-6400
Telex: 89-2537 EMBARG WSH

Australia

American Embassy Commercial Section
Moonah Pl.
Canberra, A.C.T. 2600, Australia
APO San Francisco 96404
Phone: (062)705000
Telex: 62104 USAEMB

American Consulate General—Melbourne Commercial Section
24 Albert Rd.
South Melbourne, Victoria 3205
Australia
APO San Francisco 96405
Phone: (03)699-2244
Telex: 30982 AMERCON

American Consulate General—Sydney Commercial Section
36th Fl., T&G Tower, Hyde Park Square
Park and Elizabeth Sts.
Sydney 2000, N.S.W., Australia
APO San Francisco 96209
Phone: 221-3055
Telex: 72729

Embassy of Australia Commercial Section
1601 Massachusetts Ave., NW.
Washington, DC 20036
Phone: (202)797-3201

Bahamas

American Embassy Commercial Section
Mosmar Building
Queen St.
P.O. Box N-8197
Nassau, Bahamas
Phone: (809) 322-1181/1700
Telex: 20-138 AMEMB NS 138

Embassy of the Bahamas Commercial Section
600 New Hampshire Avenue, NW., Suite 865
Washington, DC 20037
Phone: (202)338-3940
Telex: 440244 BHMS

Belgium

American Embassy Commercial Section
27 Boulevard du Regent
B-1000 Brussels, Belgium
APO New York 09667-1000
Phone: (02)513-3830
Telex: 846-21336

American Chamber of Commerce
 in Belgium
c/o Essochem, Europe, Inc.
B-1040 Brussels, Belgium
Phone: (02)720-9130
Telex: 62788

Embassy of Belgium Commercial
 Section
3330 Garfield St., NW.
Washington, DC 20008
Phone: (202)333-6900
Telex: 89 566 AMBEL WSH

Brazil

American Embassy Commercial
 Section
Avenida das Nocoes, Lote 3
Brasilia, Brazil
APO Miami 34030
Phone: (061)223-0120
Telex: 061-1091

American Consulate General—
 Rio de Janeiro Commerical
 Section
Avenida Presidente Wilson, 147
Rio de Janeiro, Brazil
APO Miami 34030
Phone: (021)292-7117
Telex: AMCONSUL 021-21466

American Consulate General—
 Sao Paulo Commercial Section
Rua Padre Joao Manoel, 933
Caixa Postal 8063
Sao Paulo, Brazil
APO Miami 34030
Phone: (011)881-6511
Telex: 011-22183

American Chamber of Commerce
 in Brazil—Sao Paulo
Caixa Postal 1980
01051, Sao Paulo, SP—-Brazil
Phone: (011)212-3132
Telex: 1132311 CASE BR

American Chamber of Commerce
 in Brazil— Rio de Janeiro
20.040 Rio de Janiero, RJ—Brazil
Phone: 203-2477
Telex: 2123539 RJRT BR
Cable: REYNOTABA

American Chamber of Commerce
 in Brazil—Salvador
c/o TABARAMA—-Tabacos do
 Brazil Ltda.
Caixa Postal 508
40.000 Salvador, Bahia—Brazil
Phone: 241-1844

Embassy of Brazil Commercial
 Section
3006 Massachusetts Ave., NW.
Washington, DC 20008
Phone: (202)745-2700
Telex: 440371 BRASMB 89430
 BRASMB

Canada

American Embassy Commercial
 Section
100 Wellington St.
Ottawa, Canada, K1P5T1
Phone: (613)238-5335
Telex: 0533582

American Consulate General—
 Calgary Commercial Section
615 Macleod Trail S.E., Rm. 1050
Calgary, Alberta, Canada T2G 4T8
Phone: (403)266-8962
Telex: 038-21332

American Consulate General—
 Montreal Commercial Section
Suite 1122, South Tower
Place Desjardins
Montreal, Quebec
Canada, H5B1G1
Phone: (514)281-1886
Telex: 05-268751

American Consulate General—
 Toronto Commercial Section
360 University Avenue
Toronto, Ontario
Canada, M5G1S4
Phone: (416)595-1700
Telex: 065-24132

American Consulate General—
 Vancouver Commercial Section
1075 West Georgia St., 21st Floor
Vancouver, British Columbia
Canada, V6E4E9
Phone: (604)685-4311
Telex: 04-55673

Embassy of Canada Commercial
 Section
1746 Massachusetts Ave., NW.
Washington, DC 20036
Phone: 785-1400
Telex: 8 99664 DOMCAN A WSH

Chile

American Embassy Commercial
 Section
Edificio Codina
Agustinas 1343
Santiago, Chile
APO Miami 34033
Phone: 710133/90 or 710326/75
Telex: 240062-ICA-CL

American Chamber of Commerce
 in Chile
Pedro de Valdivia 291
Santiago, Chile
Phone: 223-3037
Telex: 645129 CMDLC CZ

Embassy of Chile Commercial
 Section
1732 Massachusetts Ave., NW.
Washington, DC 20036
Phone (202)785-1746

China, People's Republic Of

American Embassy Commercial
 Section
Guang Hua Lu 17
Beijing, China
FPO San Francisco 96655
Phone: 52-2033
Telex: AMEMB CN 22701

American Consulate General—
 Guangzou Commercial Section
Dong Fang Hotel
Box 100
FPO San Francisco 96659
Phone: 69900; ext. 1000

American Consulate General—
 Shanghai Commercial Section
1469 Huai Hai Middle Rd.
Box 200
FPO San Franciso 96659
Phone: 379-880

American Consulate General—
 Shenyang Commercial Section
40 Lane 4, Section 5
Sanjing St., Heping District
Box 45
FPO San Francisco 96659-0002
Phone: 2 90038/34/54/68
Telex: 80011 AMCS CN

State Contacts For Export

American Chamber of Commerce
in China
Jian Guo Hotel
Jian Guo Men Wai
Beijing, People's Republic of
China
Phone: 59-5261
Telex: 210179 GJPEK CN

Embassy of the People's Republic
of China Commercial Section
2300 Connecticut Ave., NW.
Washington, DC 20008
Phone: (202)328-2520

Columbia

American Embassy Commercial
Section
Calla 38, No. 8-61
Bogota, Colombia
APO Miami 34038
Phone: 285-1300/1688
Telex: 44843

American Chamber of Commerce
in Colombia—Bogota
Trv. 18, No. 78-80
Apartado Aereo 75240
Bogota, Colombia
Phone: 256-8800
Telex: 44635

American Chamber of Commerce
in Colombia—Cali
Apartado Aereo 101
Cali, Valle, Colombia
Phone: 689-506, 689-409
Telex: 55442

Embassy of Colombia
Commercial Section
2118 Leroy Place, NW.
Washington, DC 20008
Phone: 387-8338
Telex: 197 624 COLE UT

Denmark

American Embassy Commercial
Section
Dag Hammarskjolds Alie 24
2100 Copenhagen, Denmark
APO New York 09170
Phone: (01)423144
Telex: 22216

Embassy of Denmark
Commercial Section
3200 Whitehaven, St., NW.
Washington, DC 20008
Phone: (202)234-4300
Telex: 089525 DEN EMB WSH
64444 DEN EMB WSH

Dominican Republic

American Embassy Commercial
Section
Calle Cesar Nicolas Penson con
Calle Leopoldo Navarro
Santo Domingo, Dominican
Republic
APO Miami 34041-0008
Phone: 682-2171
Telex: 3460013

American Chamber of Commerce
in the Dominican Republic
P.O. Box 1221
Santo Domingo, Dominican
Republic
Phone: 565-1661
Telex: 0034 TATEM DR

Embassy of the Dominican
Republic Commercial Section
1715 22nd St., NW.
Washington, DC 20007
Phone: (202)332-6280
Telex: 44-0031 DOR EMB

Ecuador

American Embassy Ecuador
120 Avenida Patria
Quito, Ecuador
APO Miami 34039
Phone: 548-000
Telex: 02-2329 USICAQ ED

American Consulate General—
 Guayaquil Commercial Section
9 de Octubre y Garcia Moreno
Guayaquil, Ecuador
APO Miami 34039
Phone: 511-570
Telex: 04-3452 USICAG ED

American Chamber of Commerce
 in Ecuador
P.O. Box 9103 Suc. Almagro
Quito, Ecuador
Phone: 523-152, 523-693

American Chamber of Commerce
 in Ecuador
Escobedo 1402 y Chile
P.O. Box 4767
Guayaquil, Ecuador
Phone 529-855, 516-707

Embassy of Ecuador Commercial
 Section
2535 15th St., NW.
Washington, DC 20009
Phone: (202)234-7200
Telex: 440129 ECUAI

Egypt

American Embassy Commercial
 Section
5 Sharia Latin America
Cairo, Arab Republic of Egypt
FPO New York 09527
Phone: 28219/774666
Telex: 93773 AMEMB

American Consulate General—
 Alexandria Commercial Section
110 Ave. Horreya
Alexandria, Republic of Egypt
FPO New York 09527
Phone: 801911/25607/22861/
 28458

American Chamber of Commerce
 in Egypt
Cairo Marriott Hotel, Suite 1537
P.O. Box 33 Zamalek
Cairo, Egypt
Phone: 340-8888
Telex: 20870

Embassy of Egypt Commercial
 Section
2715 Connecticut Ave., NW.
Washington, DC 20008
Phone: (202)265-9111
Telex: 89-2481 COMRAU WSH
 64-251 COMRAU WSH

France

American Embassy Commercial
 Section
1 Ave. Gabriel
75382 Paris Cedex 08
Paris, France
APO New York 09777
Phone: 96-1202/261-8075
Telex: 650-221

American Consulate General—
 Marseille Commercial Section
No. 9 Rue Armeny 13006
13006 Marseille, France
Phone: 54-92-00
Telex: 430597

American Consulate General—
 Strasbourg Commercial Section
15 Ave. D'Alsacr
67082 Strasbourg, Cedex
Strasbourg, France
APO New York 09777
Phone: (88)35-31-04/05/06
Telex: 870907

American Chamber of Commerce
 in France
53, Ave. Montaigne
75008 Paris, France
Phone: (1)359-2349

Embassy of France Commercial
 Section
4101 Reservoir Rd., NW.
Washington, DC 20007
Phone: (202)944-6000
Telex: 248320 FRCC UR

Germany (West)

American Embassy Commercial
 Section
Deichmanns Ave.
5300 Bonn 2, Germany
APO New York 09080
Phone: (0228)339-3390
Telex: 885-452

American Mission—Berline
 Commercial Section
Clayallee 170
D-1000 Berline 33 (Dahlem),
Germany
APO New York 09742
Phone: (030)819-7561
Telex: 183-701 USBER-D

American Consulate General—
 Dusseldorf Commercial Section
Cecilienalle 5
4000 Dusseldorf 30,
Germany
APO New York 09711

American Consulate General—
 Frankfurt am Main Commercial
 Section
Siesmayerstrasse 21
6000 Frankfurt
Germany
APO New York 09213
Phone: (0611) 740071
Telex: 412589 USCON-D

American Consulate General—
 Hamburg Commercial Section
Alsterufer 27/28
2000 Hamburg 36,
Germany
APO New York 09215-0002
Phone: (040)44-1061
Telex: 213777

American Consulate General—
 Munich Commercial Section
Koeniginstrasse 5
8000 Muenchen 22
APO New York 09108,
Germany
Phone: (089)23011
Telex: 5-22697 ACGM D

American Consulate General—
 Stuttgart Commercial Section
Urbanstrasse 7
7000 Stuttgart, Germany
APO New York 09154
Phone: (0711)210221
Telex: 07-22945

American Chamber of Commerce
 in Germany
Flying Tigers
Flughafen, Luftfrachtzentrum
6000 Frankfurt 75, Germany

Hong Kong

American Consulate General—
 Hong Kong Commercial Section
Hong Kong
FPO San Francisco 96659-0002
Phone: 239011
Telex: 63141 USDOC HX

American Chamber of Commerce
 in Hong Kong
Lark International, Ltd.
15/F World Commerce Center
Harbour City, 11 Canton Road
TST Kowloon, Hong Kong
Phone: 5-26595

Hong Kong Office/British
 Embassy
3100 Massachusetts Ave., NW.
Washington, DC 20008
Phone: (202)898-4591
Telex: 440484 HK WSH UY

India

American Embassy Commercial
 Section
Shanti Path, Chanakyapuri
11021 New Delhi, India
Phone: 600651
Telex: USCS IN 031-4589

American Consulate General—
 Bombay Commercial Section
Lincoln House
78 Bhulabhai Desai Road
Bombay 400026, India
Phone: 822611/8
Telex: 011-6525 ACON IN

American Consulate General—
 Calcutta Commercial Section
5/1 Ho Chi Minh Sarani
Calcutta 700071, India
Phone: 44-3611/6
Telex: 021-2483

American Consulate General—
 Madras Commercial Section
Mount Road
Madras 600006, India
Phone: 8304116

Embassy of India Commercial
 Section
2536 Massachusetts Ave., NW.
Washington, DC 20008
Phone: (202)939-7000

Indonesia

American Embassy Commercial
 Section
Medan merdeka Selatan 5
Jakarta, Indonesia
APO San Francisco 96356
Phone: 340001-9
Telex: 44218 AMEMB JKT

American Consulate— Medan
 Commercial Section
Jalan Imam Bonjol 13
Medan, Indonesia
APO San Francisco 96356
Phone: 322200
Telex: 51764

American Consulate—Surbaya
 Commercial Section
Jalan Raya Dr. Dutomo 33
Surabaya, Indonesia
APO San Francisco 96356
Phone: 69287/8
Telex: 031-334

American Chamber of Commerce
 in Indonesia
Citibank Building, 8th Pl.
Jalan M.H. Thamrin 55
Jakarta, Indonesia
Telex: 48116 CIBSEM IA

Embassy of Indonesia
  Commercial Section
2020 Massachusetts Avenue, NW.
Washington, DC 20036
Phone: (202)293-1745

Iraq

American Interests Commercial
  Section
Belgian Embassy
Opp. For. Ministry Club
Masbah Quarter
P.O. Box 2447 Alwiyah
Baghdad, Iraq
Phone: 719-6138/9
Telex: 212287 USINT IK

Embassy of Iraq Commercial
  Section
1801 P St., NW.
Washington, DC 20036
Phone: (202)483-7500
Telex: 64437 IRAQI YA
  64464 IRAQI YA

Ireland

American Embassy Commercial
  Section
42 Elgin Rd.
Ballsbridge
Dublin, Ireland
Phone: 688777
Telex: 25240

American Chamber of Commerce
  in Ireland
20 College Green
Dublin 2, Ireland
Phone: 712733
Telex: 31187 UCIL/EI

Embassy of Ireland Commercial
  Section
2234 Massachusetts Avenue, NW.
Washington, DC 20008
Phone: (202)462-3939
Telex: 64160 HIBERNIA 64160
  440419 HIBERNIA 440419

Israel

American Embassy Commercial
  Section
71 Hayarkon St.
Tel Aviv, Israel
APO New York 09672
Phone: 03-654338
Telex: 33376

American Chamber of Commerce
  in Israel
35 Shaul Hamelech Blvd.
P.O. Box 33174
Tel Aviv, Israel
Phone: (03)252341/2
Telex: 32139 BETAM IL

Embassy of Israel Commercial
  Section
1621 22nd St., NW.
Washington, DC 20008
Phone: (202)364-5400

Italy

American Embassy Commercial
  Section
Via Veneto 119/A
00187 Rome, Italy
APO New York 09794
Phone: (6)46742
Telex: 610450 AMBRMA

American Consulate General—
  Milan Commercial Section
Plazza Repubblica 32
20124 Milano
c/o U.S. Embassy
Box M
APO New York 09794
Phone: 498-2241/2/3

American Chamber of Commerce
  in Italy
c/o Peat, Marwick, Mitchell & Co.
Via San Paolo 15
20121 Milano, Italy

Embassy of Italy Commercial
  Section
1601 Fuller St., NW.
Washington, DC 20009
Phone: (202)328-5500
Telex: 90-4076 ITALY EMB WSH

Japan

American Embassy Commercial
  Section
10-1 Akasaka, 1-chome
Minato-ku (107)
Tokyo, Japan
APO San Francisco 96503
Phone: 583-7141
Telex: 2422118

American Consulate General—
  Osaka Commercial Section
Sankei Building, 9th Floor
4-9, Umeda 2-chome
Kita-ku
Osaka (530), Japan
APO San Francisco 96503
Phone: (06)341-2754/7

American Consulate—
  Fukuoka Commercial Section
5-26 Ohori 2-chome
Chuo-ku
Fukuoka (810), Japan
Box 10
FPO Seattle 98766
Phone: (092)751-9331/4
Telex: 725679

American Chamber of Commerce
  in Japan-Tokyo
c/o Burroughs Company Ltd.
13-1, Shimomiyabicho
Shinjuku-ku
Tokyo (162), Japan
Phone: 03-235-3327
Telex: 2322378 Burtok J

American Chamber of Commerce
  in Japan-Okinawa
P.O. Box 235, Koza
Okinawa City (904), Japan
Phone: 098935-2684
Telex: J79873 NANSEI OK
Cable: AMCHAM OKINAWA

Embassy of Japan Commercial
  Section
2520 Massachusetts, Ave., NW.
Washington, DC 20008
Phone: (202)234-2266
Telex: 89 540

Kuwait

American Embassy Commercial
  Section
P.O. Box 77 SAFAT
Kuwait
Phone: 424-151 through 9

American Chamber of
  Commerce in Kuwait
P.O. Box 77 Safat
Kuwait City, Kuwait
Phone: 2555597
Telex: 46902 SGT CNT KT

Embassy of Kuwait Commercial
  Section
2940 Tilden St., NW.
Washington, DC 20008
Phone: (202)966-0702
Telex: 64142 KUWAIT WSH

Malaysia

American Embassy Commercial
  Section
AIA Building 376 Jalan Tun Razak
P.O. Box 10035
Kuala Lumpur, 01-02, Malaysia
Phone: 489011
Telex: FCSKL MA 32956

American Chamber of Commerce
  in Malaysia
AIA Building
P.O. Box 759
Kuala Lumpur, Malaysia

Embassy of Malaysia Commercial
  Section
2401 Massachusetts Ave., NW.
Washington, DC 20008
Phone: (202)328-2700
Telex: 440119 MAEM UI
  61435 MALAYEM 61435

Mexico

American Embassy Commercial
  Section
Paseo de la Reforma 305
Mixico 5 D.F., Mexico
Phone: (525)21 1-0042
Telex: 017-73-091 or 017-75-685

American Consulate General—
  Guadalajara Commercial Section
Progreso 175
Guadalajara, Jal., Mexico
Phone: 25-29-98/25-27-00
Telex: 068-2-860

American Consulate General—
  Monterrey Commercial Section
Avenida Constitucion
411 Poniente
Monterrey, N.L., Mexico
Phone: 4306 50/59
Telex: 0382853

American Chamber of Commerce
  in Mexico—Mexico City
Embotelladora Tarahumara, S.A.
  de C.V.
Rio Amazonas No. 43
06500 Mexico, D.F., Mexico
Phone: 591-0066
Telex: 1775481 CCDFME

American Chamber of Commerce
  in Mexico—Guadalajara
Apartado 31-72
45070 Guadalajara, Jal., Mexico
Phone: 15-88-22

American Chamber of Commerce in
  Mexico—Monterrey
Apartado 2781
Monterrey, N.L., Mexico

Embassy of Mexico Commercial
  Section
2829 16th St., NW.
Washington, DC 20009
Phone: (202)234-6000
Telex: 90 4307 OCCMEX

Netherlands

American Embassy Commercial
  Section
Lange Voorhout 102
The Hague, the Netherlands
APO New York 09159
Phone: (070)62-49-11
Telex: (044)3106

American Consulate General—
  Amsterdam Commercial Section
Museumplein 19
Amsterdam, the Netherlands
APO New York 09159
Phone: (020)790321
Telex: 044-16176 CGUSA NL

American Consulate General—
  Rotterdam Commercial Section
Baan 50
Rotterdam, the Netherlands
APO New York 09159
Phone: (010)117560
Telex: 044-22388

The American Chamber of
  Commerce in the Netherlands
2517 KJ The Hague, the
  Netherlands
Phone: 023-339020
Telex: 41219

Embassy of the Netherlands
  Commercial Section
4200 Linnean Ave., NW.
Washington, DC 20008
Phone: (202)244-5300

Netherland Antilles

American Consulate General—
  Netherland Antilles
  Commercial Section
St. Anna Blvd. 19
P.O. Box 158
Willemstad, Curacao,
  Netherland Antilles
Phone: (5999)613066/
  613350/613441
Telex: 1062 AMCON NA

New Zealand

American Embassy Commercial
  Section
29 Fitzherbert Terr., Thorndon
Wellington, New Zealand
FPO San Francisco 96690-0001
Phone: 722-068
Telex: NZ 3305

The American Chamber of
  Commerce in New Zealand
P.O. Box 33-246 Takapuna
Auckland 9, New Zealand
Phone: 444-4760
Telex: NZ 2601

Embassy of New Zealand
  Commercial Section
37 Observatory Circle, NW.
Washington, DC 20008
Phone: (202)328-4800
Telex: 8 9526 TOTARA WSH

Nigeria

American Embassy Commercial
   Section
2 Eleke Crescent
P.O. Box 554
Lagos, Nigeria
Phone: 610097
Telex: 21670 USATO NG

American Consulate General—
   Kaduna Commercial Section
2 Maska Rd.
P.O. Box 170
Kaduna, Nigeria
Phone: (062) 213043/
   213074/213175

Embassy of Nigeria Commercial
   Section
2201 M St., NW.
Washington, DC 20037
Phone: (202)822-1500
Telex: 89 2311 NIGERIAN WSH

Norway

American Embassy Commercial
   Section
Drammensveien 18
Oslo 2, Norway
APO New York 09085
Phone: 44-85-50
Telex: 18470

Embassy of Norway Commercial
   Section
2720 34th St., NW.
Washington, DC 20008
Phone: 333-6000
Telex: 89-234 NORAMB WSH

Pakistan

American Embassy Commercial
   Section
Diplomatic Enclave, Ramna 5
P.O. Box 1048
Islamabad, Pakistan
Phone: 8261-61 through 79
Telex: 825-864

American Consulate General—
   Karachi, Pakistan
8 Abdullah Haroon Rd.
Karachi, Pakistan
Phone: 515081
Telex: 82-02-611

American Consulate General
50 Zafar Ali Road
Gulberg 5
Lahore, Pakistan
Phone: 870221 through 5

American Chamber of
   Commerce in Pakistan
3rd Floor, Shaheen Commercial
   Complex
G.P.O. 1322
M.R. Kayani Rd.
Karachi, Pakistan
Phone: 526436
Telex: 25620 CHASE PK

Embassy of Pakistan Commercial
   Section
2315 Massachusettts Ave., NW.
Washington, DC 20008
Phone: (202)939-6200
Telex: 89-2348 PARAP WSH

Panama

American Embassy Commercial
  Section
Avenida Balboa y Calle 38
Apartado 6959

Panama 5, Republic of Panama
Box E
APO Miami 34002
Phone: Panama 27-1777

American Chamber of Commerce
  in Panama
Apartado 5010
Panama 5, Republic of Panama
Phone: 60-0122

Embassy of Panama Commercial
  Section
2862 McGill Terr., NW.
Washington, DC 20008
Phone: (202)483-1407

Peru

American Embassy Commercial
  Section
Grimaldo Del Solar 358
Miraflores, Lima 18, Peru
APO Miami 34031
Phone: 44-3921
Telex: 25028PE USCOMATT

American Chamber of Commerce
  in Peru
3M Peru, S.A.
P.O. Box 1897
Lima 100, Peru

Embassy of Peru Commercial
  Section
1700 Massachusetts Ave., NW.
Washington, DC 20036
Phone: (202)833-9860
Telex: 197675 LEPRU UT

Philippines

American Embassy Commercial
  Section
395 Buendia Ave.
Extension Makati
Manila, the Philippines
APO San Francisco 96528
Phone: 818-6674
Telex: 66887 COSEC PN

American Chamber of Commerce
  in the Philippines
P.O. Box 1578 MCC
Makati
Philippines, Manila
Phone: 819-7911
Telex: (RCA)63637 SDTCO PN

Embassy of the Philippines
  Commercial Section
1617 Massachusetts Ave., NW.
Washington, DC 20036
Phone: (202)483-1414
Telex: 44 0059 AMBPHIL

Portugal

American Embassy Commercial
  Section
Ave. das Forcas Armadas
1600 Lisbon, Portugal
APO New York 09678-0002
Phone: 726-6600
Telex: 12528 AMEMB

American Chamber of Commerce
  in Portugal
Ave. Marcechal Gomes de Costa
  33
1800 Lisbon, Portugal
Phone: 853996
Telex: 12599 AUTOREX P

State Contacts For Export

Embassy of Portugal Commercial
Section
2125 Kalorama Rd., NW.
Washington, DC 20008
Phone: (202)328-8610
Telex: 64399 PORT EMB P

Saudi Arabia

American Embassy Commercial
Section
Sulaimaniah District
P.O. Box 9041
Riyadh, Saudi Arabia
APO New York 09038
Phone: (01)464-0012
Telex: 201363 USRIAD SJ

American Consulate General—
Dhahran Commercial Section
Between Aramco Headquarters
and Dhahran International
Airport
P.O. Box 81, Dhahran Airport
Dhahran, Saudi Arabia
APO New York 09616
Phone: (03)8913200
Telex: 601925 AMCON SJ

American Consulate General—
Jeddah Commercial Section
Palestine Rd., Ruwais
P.O. Box 149
Jeddah, Saudi Arabia
APO New York 09697
Phone: (02)667-0080
Telex: 401459 AMEMB SJ

The American Businessmen of
Jeddah, Saudi Arabia
P.O. Box 5019
Jeddah, Saudi Arabia
Phone: 651-7968
Telex: 401906 UCAJED SJ

American Chamber of Commerce
in Saudi Arabia
c/o Saudi Business Systems
P.O. Box 4992
Dhahran, Saudi Arabia
Phone: 864-5838, 894-8181
Telex: 670418 SABSYS SJ

Embassy of Saudi Arabia
Commercial Section
601 New Hampshire Ave., NW.
Washington, DC 20037
Phone: (202)483-2100

Singapore

American Embassy Commercial
Section
30 Hill St.
Singapore 0617
FPO San Francisco 96699-0001
Phone: 338-0251

American Chamber of Commerce
in Singapore
11 Dhoby Ghaut
08-04 Cathay Building
Sinagpore 0922

Embassy of Singapore
Commercial Section
1824 R. St., NW.
Washington, DC 20009
Phone: (202)667-7555
Telex: 440024 SING EMB

South Africa

American Consulate General
Johannesburg Commercial
Section
Kine Center, 11th Floor
Commissioner and Krulis Sts.
P.O. Box 2155
Johannesburg, South Africa
Phone: (011)331-1681
Telex: 48-3780-SA

American Chamber of Commerce
 in South Africa
P.O. Box 1616
Johannesburg 2000, South Africa

Embassy of South Africa
 Commercial Section
4801 Massachusetts Ave., NW.
Washington, DC 20016
Phone: 966-1650

South African Consulate
 General—Commercial Section
425 Park Ave.
New York, NY 10022
Phone: (212)838-1700
Telex: 233290

South Korea

American Embassy Commercial
 Section
82 Sejong-Ro; Chongro-ku
Korea
APO San Francisco 96301
Phone: 732-2601 through 18
Telex: AMEMB 23108

Embassy of Korea
2320 Massachusetts Ave., NW.
Washington, DC 20008

Spain

American Embassy Commercial
 Section
Serrano 75
Madrid, Spain
APO New York 09285
Phone: 276-3400/3600
Telex: 27763

American Consulate General—
 Barcelona Commercial Section
Via Layetana
Barcelona, Spain
Box 5
APO New York 09285
Phone: 319-9550
Telex: 52672

American Chamber of Commerce
 in Spain
Paseo de Gracia 95
Barcelona 8, Spain

Embassy of Spain Commercial
 Section
2558 Massachusetts Ave., NW.
Washington, DC 20008
Phone: (202)265-8600
Telex: 89 2747 SPAIN WSH

Sweden

American Embassy Commercial
 Section
Strandvagen 101
Stockholm, Sweden
Phone: (08)63.05.20
Telex: 12060 AMEMB S

Embassy of Sweden Commercial
 Section
600 New Hampshire Ave., NW.
Washington, DC 20037
Phone: (202)298-3500
Telex: 89 2724 SVENSK WSH

Switzerland

American Embassy Commercial
 Section
Jubilaeumstrasse 93
3005 Bern, Switzerland
Phone: (031)437011
Telex: (845)32128

State Contacts For Export

American Chamber of Commerce
 in Switzerland
Bahnhofstrasse 45
8021 Zurich, Switzerland
Phone: 2112454
Telex: 812747 Ipco Ch

Embassy of Switzerland
 Commercial Section
2900 Cathedral Ave., NW.
Washington, DC 20008
Phone: (202)745-7900
Telex: 64180 AMSWIS

Taiwan

American Chamber of Commerce
 in Taiwan
P.O. Box 17-277
Taipei, Taiwan, R.O.C.

American Institute in Taiwan
 (AIT)
1700 N. Moore St.
17th Floor
Arlington, VA 22209
Phone: (703)525-8474

American Institute in Taiwan
 (AIT)
7 Lane 134 Hsin Yi Rd.
Section 3
Taipei, Taiwan
Telex: 23890 USTRADE

Coordination Council for
 North American Affairs
Economic Division
4301 Connecticut Ave., NW.
Suite 420
Washington, DC 20008
Phone: (202)686-6400
Telex: 440292 SINOECO

USA-ROC Economic Council
200 South Main St.
P.O. Box 517
Crystal Lake, IL 60014
Phone: (815)459-5875

Thailand

American Embassy Commercial
 Section
Shell Building, R Floor
140 Wireless Rd.
Bangkok, Thailand
APO San Francisco 96346
Phone: 251-9260/2
Telex: 20966 FCSBKK

American Chamber of Commerce
 in Thailand
4th Floor, Wanglee Building
297 Suriwongse Rd.
Bangkok 10500, Thailand
Phone: 234-5173
Telex: LYMAN TH 82978

Embassy of Thailand Commercial
 Section
1990 M St., NW., Suite 350
Washington, DC 20036
Phone: (202)467-6790
Telex: 248 275 TTHAI UR

Trinidad & Tobago

American Embassy Commercial
 Section
15 Queen's Park West
P.O. Box 752

Port-of-Spain, Trinidad, and
 Tobago
Phone: 62-26371
Telex: 22230 AMEMB POS

Embassy of Trinidad and
Tobago Commercial Section
1708 Massachusetts Ave., NW.
Washington, DC 20036
Phone: (202)467-6490
Telex: 64321 TRINOFF

Turkey

American Embassy Commercial
Section
110 Ataturk Blvd.
Ankara, Turkey
APO New York 09254
Phone: 265470
Telex: 43144 USIA TR

American Consulate General—
Istanbal Commercial Section
104-108 Mesrutiyet Caddesi
Tepebasl
Istanbal, Turkey
APO New York 09380
Phone: 1436200/09
Telex: 24306 USIC TR

Embassy of Turkey Commercial
Section
2523 Massachusetts Ave., NW.
Washington, DC 20008
Phone: (202)483-6366
Telex: 904143 TURKFIN

Union Of Soviet Socialist Republic

American Embassy Commercial
Section
Ulitsa Chazkovskogo 19/21/23
Moscow, Union of Soviet Socialist
Republic
APO New York 09862
Phone: (096) 252-24-51 through 59
Telex: 413160 USGSO SU

U.S. Commercial Office—Moscow
Ulitsa Chaykovskogo 15
Moscow, U.S.S.R.
APO New York 09862
Phone: 001-7-95-255-46-60
Telex: 413-205 USCO SU

U.S.S.R. Trade Representative in
the U.S.A.
2001 Connecticut Ave., NW.
Washington, DC 20008
Phone: (202)232-2917

United Arab Emirates

American Chamber of Commerce
in U.A.E.
P.O. Box 155
Dubai, United Arab Emirates
Phone: 971-4-442790
Telex: 45544 CALTX

American Embassy Commercial
Section
United Bank Bldg., Flat No. 702
Corner of Liwa St., and
Corniche Rd.
Abu Dhabi, U.A.E.
Phone: 345545
Telex: 22229 AMEMBY EM

American Embassy Branch
Office— Dubai Commercial
Section
Dubai International Trade Center
P.O. Box 9343
Dubai, U.A.E.
Phone: 471115
Telex: 98346031 BACCUS EM

Embassy of the United Arab
Emirates Commercial Section
600 New Hampshire Ave., NW.,
Suite 740
Washington, DC 20037
Phone: (202)338-6500

United Kingdom

American Embassy Commercial Section
24/31 Grosvenor Square
London W. 1A 1AE, England
Box 40
FPO New York 09510
Phone: (01)499-9000
Telex: 266777

American Chamber of Commerce in the United Kingdom
c/o The Chase Manhatten Bank, NA
Woolgate HSE.
Coleman St.
London EC2P 2HD, United Kingdom
Phone: 01-726-5000
Telex: 8954681 CMBG

Embassy of Great Britain Commercial Section
3100 Massachusetts Ave., NW.
Washington, DC 20008
Phone: (202)462-1340
Telex: 892384 WSH
892380 WSH

Venezuela

American Embassy Commercial Section
Avenida Francisco de Miranda and Avenida Principal de la Floresta
P.O. Box 62291
Caracas 1060 A, Venezuela
APO Miami 34037
Phone: 284-7111/6111
Telex: 25501 AMEMB VE

American Chamber of Commerce in Venezuela
Apartado 5991
Caracas 1010-A, Venezuela
Phone: 241-0882, 241-4705
Telex: 25214

Embassy of Venezuela Commercial Section
2445 Massachusetts Ave., NW.
Washington, DC 20015
Phone: (202)797-3800

APPENDIX B

EXPORT GLOSSARY

Acceptance—This term has several related meanings:
1. A time draft (or bill of exchange) which the drawee has accepted and is unconditionally obligated to pay at maturity. The draft must be presented first for acceptance—the drawee becomes the "acceptor"—then for payment. The word "accepted" and the date and place of payment must be written on the face of the draft.
2. The drawee's act in receiving a draft and thus entering into the obligation to pay its value at maturity.
3. Broadly speaking, any agreement to purchase goods under specified terms. An agreement to purchase goods at a stated price and under stated terms.

Ad valorem—According to value. *See* Duty.

Advance against document—A loan made on the security of the documents covering the shipment.

Advising bank—A bank, operating in the exporter's country, that handles letters of credit for a foreign bank by notifying the exporter that the credit has been opened in his/her favor. The advising bank fully informs the exporter of the conditions of the letter of credit without necessarily bearing responsibility for payment.

Advisory capacity—A term indicating that a shipper's agent or representative is not empowered to make definitive decisions or adjustments without approval of the group or individual represented. *Compare* Without reserve.

Agent—*See* Foreign sales agent.

Agio—The premium paid to exchange one currency for another.

Air waybill—A bill of lading that covers both domestic and international flights transporting goods to a specified destination. This is a non-negotiable instrument of air transport that serves as a receipt for the shipper, indicating that the carrier has accepted the goods listed and obligates itself to carry the consignment to the airport of destination according to specified conditions. *Compare* Inland bill of lading, Ocean bill of lading, and Through bill of lading.

Allenge—A slip of paper attached to a bill of exchange, acceptance or note, providing space for additional endorsements.

Alongside—A phrase referring to the side of a ship. Goods to be delivered "alongside" are to be placed on the dock or barge within reach of the transport ship's tackle so that they can be loaded aboard the ship.

Antidiversion clause—*See* Destination control statement.

A/P—*See* Authority to pay.

Arbitrage—The process of buying foreign exchange, stocks, bonds, and other commodities in one market and immediately selling them in another market at higher prices.

Asian dollars—U.S. dollars deposited in Asia and the Pacific Basin. *Compare* Eurodollars.

Authority to pay—A letter, used primarily in the Far East, addressed by a bank to a seller of merchandise, authorizing the purchase, with or without recourse, of draft(s) and document(s) to a stipulated amount drawn on a foreign buyer in payment of specified merchandise shipment(s).

Back-to-back credit—A term used to denote a letter of credit issued for the account of a buyer of merchandise already holding a letter of credit in his favor. The "back-to-back" letter of credit is issued in favor of the supplier of the merchandise to cover the same shipment stipulated in the credit already held by the buyer. The terms of both letters of credit, with the exception of the amount and expiration date, are so similar that the same documents presented under "back-to-back" credit are subsequently applied against the credit in favor of the buyer. However, the buyer or beneficiary of the first draft substitutes his draft and invoice for those presented by the supplier.

Balance of trade—The difference between a country's total imports and exports. If exports exceed imports, a favorable balance of trade exists; if not, a trade deficit is said to exist.

Barter—Trade in which merchandise is exchanged directly for other merchandise without the use of money. Barter is an important means of trade with countries using currency that is not readily convertible.

Export Glossary 221

Beneficiary—The person in whose favor a letter of credit is issued or a draft is drawn.

Bill of exchange—*See* Draft.

Bill of lading—A document that establishes the terms of a contract between a shipper and a transportation company under which freight is to be moved between specified points for a specified charge. Usually prepared by the shipper on forms issued by the carrier, it serves as a document of title, a contract of carriage, and a receipt for goods. *Also see* Air waybill, Inland bill of lading, Ocean bill of lading, and Through bill of lading.

Binder—A temporary insurance coverage pending the later issuance of an insurance policy or certificate.

Bonded warehouse—A warehouse authorized by Customs authorities for storage of goods on which payment of duties is deferred until the goods are removed.

Booking—An arrangement with a steamship company for the acceptance and carriage of freight.

Buying agent—*See* Purchasing agent.

C&F—*See* Cost & freight.

C&I—*See* Cost & insurance.

Carnet—A customs document permitting the holder to carry or send merchandise temporarily into certain foreign countries for display, demonstration, or similar purposes without paying duties or posting bonds.

Cash against documents (C.A.D.)—Payment for goods in which a commission house or other intermediary transfers title documents to the buyer upon payment in cash.

Cash in advance (C.I.A.)—Payment for goods in which the price is paid in full before shipment is made. This method is usually used only for small purchases or when the goods are built to order.

Cash with order (C.W.O.)—Payment for goods in which the buyer pays when ordering and in which the transaction is binding on both parties.

Certificate of inspection—A document certifying that merchandise (perishable goods, for example) was in good condition immediately prior to its shipment.

Certificate of manufacture—A statement (often notarized) in which a producer of goods certifies that manufacture has been completed and that the goods are now at the disposal of the buyer.

Certificate of origin—A document, required by certain foreign countries for tariff purposes, certifying the country of origin of specified goods.

Charges forward—A banking term used when foreign and domestic bank commission charges, interest, and government taxes in connection with the collection of a draft are credited to the drawee's account.

Appendix B

Charges here—A written contract, usually on a special form, between the owner of a vessel and a "charterer" who rents use of the vessel or a part of its freight space. The contract generally includes the freight rates and the ports involved in the transportation.

C.I.F.—*See* Cost, insurance, freight.

Clean bill of lading—A receipt for goods issued by a carrier that indicated that the goods were received in "apparent good order and condition," without damages or other irregularities. *Compare* Foul bill of lading.

Clean draft—A draft to which no documents have been attached.

Collection papers—All documents (commercial invoices, bills of lading, etc.) submitted to a buyer for the purpose of receiving payment for a shipment.

Commercial attaché—The commerce expert on the diplomatic staff of his/her country's embassy or large consulate.

Commercial invoice—An itemized list of goods shipped, usually included among an exporter's collection papers.

Commission agent—*See* Purchasing agent.

Common carrier—An individual, partnership or corporation that transports persons or goods for compensation.

Confirmed letter of credit—A letter of credit, issued by a foreign bank, with validity confirmed by a U.S. bank. An exporter who requires a confirmed letter of credit from the buyer is assured of payment by the U.S. bank even if the foreign buyer or the foreign bank defaults. *See* Letter of credit.

Consignee—The person, firm, or representative to which a seller or shipper sends merchandise.

Consignment—Delivery of merchandise from an exporter (the consignor) to an agent (the consignee) under agreement that the agent sell the merchandise for the account of the exporter. The consignor retains title to the goods until the consignee has sold them. The consignee sells the goods for commission and remits the net proceeds to the consignor.

Consignor—The seller or shipper of merchandise.

Consular declaration—A formal statement, made to the consul of a foreign country, describing goods to be shipped.

Consular documents—Bills of lading, certificates of origin, or special invoice forms that are officially signed by the consul of the country of destination.

Consular invoice—A document, required by some foreign countries, describing a shipment of goods and showing information such as the consignor, consignee, and value of the shipment. Certified by a consular official of the foreign country, it is used by the country's customs officials to verify the value, quantity and nature of the shipment.

Consular visa—An official signature that the consul of the country of destination affixes to certain shipping documents.

Convertible currency—A currency that can be bought and sold for other currencies at will.

Correspondent bank—A bank that, in its own country, handles the business of a foreign bank.

Cost and freight (C&F)—A pricing term indicating that the cost of the goods and freight charges are included in the quoted price. The buyer arranges for and pays for the insurance.

Cost and insurance (C&I)—A pricing term indicating that the cost of the product and insurance are included in the quoted price. The buyer is responsible for freight to the named port of destination.

Cost, insurance, freight (C.I.F.)—A pricing term indicating that the cost of the goods, insurance, and freight are included in the quoted price.

Countertrade—The sale of goods or services that are paid for in whole or in part by the transfer of goods or services from a foreign country. *See* Barter.

Cover note—The british equivalent of the U.S. "binder."

Credit risk insurance—Insurance designed to cover risks of nonpayment for delivered goods.

Customs—The authorities designated to collect duties levied by a country on imports and exports. The term also applies to the procedures involved in such collection.

Customhouse broker—An individual or firm licensed to enter and clear goods through Customs.

Date draft—A draft that matures in a specified number of days after the date on which it is issued, without regard to the date of acceptance. *See* Draft, Sight draft and Time draft.

Deferred payment credit—Type of letter of credit providing for payment some time after presentation of shipping documents by exporter.

Delivery order—An order issued to or by a warehouse, railroad, airline, or steamship company, or anyone with the authority and legal right to claim or order delivery of merchandise.

Demand draft—*See* Sight draft.

Destination control statement—Any of various statements that the U.S. government requires to be displayed on export shipments and that specify the destinations for which export of the shipment has been authorized.

Devaluation—The official lowering of the value of one country's currency in terms of one or more foreign currencies.

Discount—In two forms:
    a. Commercial: an allowance from the quoted price of goods, usually made by the deduction of a certain percentage from the invoice price.

b. Financial: a deduction from the face value of commercial paper, such as bills of exchange and acceptances, in consideration of receipt by the seller of cash before maturity date.

Discrepancy - Letter of Credit—When documents presented do not conform to the letter of credit, it is referred to as a "discrepancy."

Dispatch—An amount paid by a vessel's operator to a charterer if loading or unloading is completed in less time than stipulated in the charter party.

Distributor—A foreign agent who sells for a supplier directly and maintains an inventory of the supplier's products.

Dock receipt—A receipt issued by an ocean carrier to acknowledge receipt of a shipment at the carrier's dock or warehouse. *See* Warehouse receipt.

Documentary credit—A commercial letter of credit providing for payment by a bank to the name beneficiary, usually the seller of merchandise, against delivery of documents specified in the credit.

Documentary draft—A draft to which documents are attached.

Documents against acceptance (D/A)—Instructions given by a shipper to a bank indicating that documents transferring title to goods should be delivered to the buyer (or drawee) only upon the buyer's acceptance of the attached draft.

Documents against payment (D/P)—Instructions a shipper gives to his/her bank that the documents attached to a draft for collection are deliverable to the drawee only against his payment of the draft.

Draft—An unconditional order in writing from one person (the drawer) to another (the drawee) directing the drawee to pay a specified amount to a named drawer at a fixed or determinable future date. *See* Date draft, Sight draft, Time draft.

Drawback—Articles manufactured or produced in the U.S. with the use of imported components or raw materials and later exported are entitled to a refund of up to 99 percent of the duty charged on the imported components. The refund of duty is known as a "drawback."

Drawee—The individual or firm on whom a draft is drawn and who owes the stated amount. *Compare* Drawer. *See* Draft.

Drawer—The individual or firm that issues or signs a draft and thus stands to receive payment of the stated amount from the drawee. *Compare* Drawee. *See* Draft.

Drop ship—Shipment by foreign shipper directly to your domestic customer. Price includes freight and postage.

Dumping—Exporting/importing merchandise into a country below the costs incurred in production and shipment.

Duty—A tax imposed on imports by the customs authority of a country. Duties are generally based on the value of the goods (ad valorem duties), some other factor such as weight or quantity (specific duties), or a combination of value and other factors (compound duties).

EMC—*See* Export management company.

ETC—*See* Export trading company.

Eurodollars—U.S. dollars placed on deposit in banks outside the United States. Usually refers to deposits in Europe.

Ex-"From"—When used in pricing terms such as "Ex Factory" or "Ex Dock," it signifies that the price quoted applies only at the point of origin (e.g., the seller's factory or a dock at the import point). In practice, this kind of quotation indicates that the seller agrees to place the goods at the disposal of the buyer at the specified place within a fixed period of time.

Exchange permit—A government permit sometimes required by the importer's government to enable the importer to convert his/her own country's currency into foreign currency with which to pay a seller in another country.

Exchange rate—The price of one currency in terms of another currency.

Eximbank—The Export-Import Bank of the United States.

Export broker—An individual or firm that brings together buyers and sellers for a fee but does not take part in actual sales transactions.

Export commission house—An organization which, for a commission, acts as a purchasing agent for a foreign buyer.

Export declaration—*See* Shipper's export declaration.

Export license—A government document that permits the licensee to engage in the export of designated goods to certain destinations. *See* General and validated licenses.

Export management company—A private firm that serves as the export department for several manufacturers, soliciting and transacting export business on behalf of its clients in return for a commission, salary, or retainer plus commission.

Export trading company—A firm similar to an export management company.

F.A.S.—*See* Free alongside.

F.I.—*See* Free in.

F.O.—*See* Free out.

F.O.B.—*See* Free on board.

Force majeure—The title of a standard clause in marine contracts exempting the parties for nonfulfillment of their obligations as a result of conditions beyond their control, such as earthquakes, floods, or war.

Foreign exchange—The currency or credit instruments of a foreign country. Also, transactions involving purchase and/or sales of currencies.

Foreign freight forwarder—*See* Freight forwarder.

Foreign sales agent—An individual of firm that serves as the foreign representative of a domestic supplier and seeks sales abroad for the supplier.

Foreign trade zone—*See* Free trade zone.

Foul bill of lading—A receipt for goods issued by a carrier with an indication that the goods were damaged when received. *Compare* Clean bill of lading.

Free alongside—A pricing term indicating that the quoted price includes the cost of delivering the goods alongside a designated vessel.

Free in—A pricing term indicating that the charterer of a vessel is responsible for the cost of loading and unloading goods from the vessel.

Free out—A pricing term indicating that the charterer of a vessel is responsible for the cost of loading goods onto the vessel.

Free on board—A pricing term indicating that the quoted price includes the cost of loading the goods into transport vessels at the specified place.

Free port—An area such as a port city into which merchandise may legally be moved without payment of duties.

Free trade zone—A port designated by the government of a country for duty-free entry of any non-prohibited goods. Merchandise may be stored, displayed, used for manufacturing, etc. within the zone and reexported without duties being paid. Duties are imposed on the merchandise (or items manufactured from the merchandise) only when the goods pass from the zone into an area of the country subject to the Customs authority.

Freight forwarder—An independent business which handles export shipments for compensation.

Future exchange contract—Usually a contract between a bank and its customer to purchase or sell foreign exchange at a fixed rate with delivery at a specified time, generally used because the customer desires to preclude the risk of fluctuations in foreign exchange rates.

General export license—Any of various export licenses covering export commodities for which *Valid export licenses* are not required. No formal application or written authorization is needed to ship exports under a General export license.

Go-down—A warehouse in the Far East where goods are stored and delivered when warranted.

Gross weight—The full weight of a shipment including goods and packaging. *Compare* Tare weight.

Import license—A document required and issued by some national governments authorizing the importation of goods into their individual countries.

In bond—A term applied to the status of merchandise admitted provisionally to a country without payment of duties—either for storage in a bonded warehouse or for trans-shipment to another point where duties eventually will be imposed.

Inland bill of lading—A bill of lading used in transporting goods overland to the exporter's international carrier. Although a Through bill of lading sometimes can be used, it usually is necessary to prepare both an Inland bill of lading and an Ocean bill of lading for export shipments. *Compare* Air waybill, Ocean bill of lading and Through bill of lading.

International freight forwarder—*See* Freight forwarder.

Irrevocable letter of credit—A letter of credit in which the specified payment is guaranteed by the bank if all terms and conditions are met by the drawee.

Letter of credit - commercial (L/C)—A document, issued by a bank per instructions by a buyer of goods, authorizing the seller to draw a specified sum of money under specified terms, usually the receipt by the bank of certain documents within a given time.

   a. Confirmed irrevocable letter of credit: A letter to which has been added the responsibility of a bank other than the issuing bank.
   b. Irrevocable letter of credit: A letter of credit which can neither be modified nor cancelled without the agreement of all concerned.
   c. Revocable letter of credit: A revocable credit may be modified or cancelled at any time without notice to the beneficiary. However, payment or acceptance made by the negotiating bank within the terms of the credit prior to receipt of cancellation from the issuing bank validly bind all concerned parties.
   d. Revolving credit: A letter from the issuing bank notifying a seller of merchandise that the amount involved when utilized will again become available, usually under the same terms and without the issuance of another letter.

Special clauses:

   a. Red clause: A clause authorizing the drawing of clean drafts without documents accompanied by a statement that pertinent shipping documents will be furnished later.
   b. Telegraphic transfer clause: A clause including an undertaking by the issuing bank to pay the draft amount to the negotiating bank upon receipt of an authenticated cablegram from the latter indicating it has received the required documents.

Letter of credit - traveler's—A letter addressed by a bank to its correspondent banks authorizing them to honor drafts of the holder to the amount of credit.

Licensing—A business arrangement in which the manufacturer of a product (or a firm with proprietary rights over certain technology, trademarks, etc.) grants permission to some other group or individual to manufacture that product (or make use of that proprietary material) in return for specified royalties or other payment.

Lighterage—The cost of loading or unloading a vessel by barges.

Manifest—*See* Ship's manifest.

Marine insurance—Insurance that compensates the owners of goods transported overseas in the event of loss that cannot be legally recovered from the carrier. Also covers air shipments. *Compare* Credit risk insurance.

Marking (or marks)—Letters, numbers, and other symbols placed on cargo packages to facilitate identification.

Ocean bill of lading—A bill of lading (B/L) indicating that the exporter consigns a shipment to an international carrier for transportation to a specified foreign market. Unlike an Inland B/L, the Ocean B/L also serves as a collection document. If it is a "straight" B/L, the foreign buyer can obtain the shipment from the carrier by simply showing proof of identity. If a "negotiable" B/L is used, the buyer must first pay for the goods, post a bond or meet other conditions agreeable to the seller. *Compare* Air waybill, Inland bill of lading and Through bill of lading.

Ocean marine insurance policy—An indemnity contract designed to reimburse an insured for the loss because of unforeseen circumstances or damage to merchandise shipped. The basic marine policy insures transportation perils but can be amended to cover additional hazards.

   a.   Open policy: A marine insurance contract in which the insurer agrees that all shipments moving at the insured's risk are automatically covered under the policy, and the insured agrees to report the shipments and to pay premium thereon to the insurer.

   b.   Special marine policy: Sometimes referred to as a marine insurance certificate, this is a policy covering a specific shipment. Most frequently, it is used to provide evidence of insurance.

Marine insurance terms:

   a.   Average: A term of marine insurance meaning loss or damage.

   b.   General average: A loss arising from a voluntary sacrifice made of any part of the vessel or cargo, or an expenditure to prevent loss of the whole and for the benefit of all persons at interest. The loss is apportioned not only among all the shippers, including those whose property is lost, but also to the vessel itself. Until the assessment is paid, a lien lies against the entire cargo.

   c.   Particular average: A marine insurance term meaning a partial loss or damage.

   d.   With average (W.A.) or With particular average (W.P.A.): Provides protection for partial loss by perils of the sea if it amounts to a certain percentage, usually three percent of the insured value. The three percent, a franchise, is not a deductible percentage but the minimum amount of claim. The franchise does not apply when a vessel is involved in a fire, stranding, sinking, burning, or collision, or in a General average loss.

   e.   Free of particular average, American conditions (FPAAC): Covers only those losses directly resulting from fire, stranding, sinking, or collision of the vessel.

   f.   Free of particular average, English conditions (FPAEC): Resembles FPAAC except that partial loss resulting from any peril of the sea becomes recoverable when the vessel has been stranded, sunk, burned, or in a collision with the insured cargo aboard. The actual damage need not result from these specific perils directly—it is only necessary that one of them has occurred.

g. Average irrespective of percentage: The broadest "with average" clause permits full recovery, regardless of percentage or of partial losses due to perils of the sea.

h. All risks: The broadest marine insurance coverage insures merchandise against all risks of physical loss or damage from any external cause which may arise.

i. Warehouse to warehouse: A common marine insurance term referring to coverage which attaches to the goods upon their leaving the shipper's warehouse and continuing during the ordinary course of transit until delivered to the consignee's warehouse, within specified time limits.

j. Both to blame collision clause: Constitutes protection against a disclaimer of liability. It appears in some bills of lading when damage results from negligence of both vessels that are parties to the accident.

k. Strikes, riots and civil commotion (SR&CC): The marine policy does not cover these risks except on endorsement.

l. Free of capture and seizure (FC&S): This excludes the risks of war and warlike operations from the policy.

m. War risk: The risks of war may be covered under a separate war-risk-only policy or by an endorsement to the Special or Individual marine policy.

On board bill of lading—A bill of lading in which a carrier certifies that goods have been placed on board a certain vessel.

Open account—A trade Arrangement in which goods are shipped to a foreign buyer without guarantee of payment. The obvious risk that this method poses to the supplier makes it essential that the buyer's integrity be unquestionable.

Order bill of lading—A negotiable bill of lading made out to the order of the shipper.

Packing list—A list showing the number and kinds of items being shipped, along with other information needed for transportation purposes.

Parcel post receipt—The postal authorities' signed acknowledgement of delivery to receiver of a shipment made by parcel post.

PEFCO—*See* Private Export Funding Corporation.

Perils of the sea—A marine insurance term used to designate heavy weather, stranding, lightning, collision, and sea water damage.

Per mille - Per 1,000—a basis upon which quotations are often made in foreign countries instead of fractional percentage. One "per mille" equals one-tenth of a percent.

Per pro—An abbreviation for per procuration, applied to the signature of an authorized agent on behalf of his/her principal.

Phytosanitary inspection certificate—A certificate issued by the U.S. Department of Agriculture to satisfy import regulations for foreign countries, it indicates that a U.S. shipment has been inspected and is free from harmful pests and plant diseases.

Political risk—In export financing, the risk of loss due to such causes as currency inconvertibility, government action preventing entry of goods, expropriation or confiscation, war, and the like.

Private Export Funding Corporation (PEFCO)—An organization that lends to foreign buyers in order to finance exports from the U.S.

Pro forma invoice—An invoice provided by a supplier prior to the shipment of merchandise that informs the buyer of the kinds and quantities of goods to be sent, their value, and such important specifications as weight, size, and so on.

Protest—Represents a certificate of dishonor provided by a consul, vice consul, notary public, or other individual suitably authorized when an instrument presented for acceptance or payment is refused.

Purchasing agent—An agent who purchases goods in his/her own country on behalf of foreign importers such as government agencies and large private concerns.

Quota—The quantity of goods of a specific kind that a country permits to be imported without restriction or imposition of additional duties.

Quotation—An offer to sell goods at a stated price and under specified conditions.

Rate of exchange—An expression signifying the basis on which the money of one country will be exchanged for that of another.

Rebate rate—The rate of percentage deductible if a bill of exchange or draft is paid before its maturity date.

Representative—*See* Foreign sales agent.

Revocable letter of credit—A letter of credit that can be cancelled or altered by the drawee (buyer) after it has been issued by the drawee's bank. *Compare* Irrevocable letter of credit.

Schedule B—Refers to "Schedule B, Statistical Classification of Domestic and Foreign Commodities Exported form the United States." All commodities exported form the U.S. must be assigned a seven-digit Schedule B number.

Shipper's export declaration—A form required by the U.S. Treasury Department for all shipments and prepared by a shipper. It indicates the value, weight, destination, and other basic information about an export shipment.

Ship's manifest—An instrument in writing, signed by the captain of a ship, that lists the individual shipments constituting the ship's cargo.

Sight draft (S/D)—A draft that is payable on presentation to the drawee. *Compare* Date draft, Time draft.

Spot exchange—The purchase or sale of foreign exchange for immediate delivery.

Export Glossary 231

Standard Industrial Classification (SIC)—A standard numerical coding system used by the U.S. government to classify products and services.

Standard International Trade Classification (SITC)—A standard numerical code developed by the United Nations to classify commodities used in international trade.

Steamship conference—A group of steamship operators that operate under mutually agreeable freight rates.

Straight bill of lading—A non-negotiable bill of lading in which the goods are consigned directly to a named consignee.

Tare weight—The weight of the container and packing materials without the weight of the goods it contains. *Compare* Gross weight.

Tenor—Designation of a payment as being due at sight, a given number of days after sight, or a given number of days after date.

Through bill of lading—A single bill of lading converting both the domestic and international carriage of an export shipment. An air waybill, for instance, is essentially a through bill of lading used for air shipments. Ocean shipments, on the other hand, usually require two separate documents, an Inland bill of lading for domestic carriage and an Ocean bill of lading for international carriage. Through bills of lading are insufficient for ocean shipments. *Compare* Air waybill, Inland bill of lading, Ocean bill of lading.

Time draft—A draft that matures either a certain number of days after acceptance or a certain number of days after the date of the draft. *Compare* Date draft, Sight draft.

Tramp steamer—A ship not operating on regular routes or schedules.

Transaction statement—A document that delineates the terms and conditions agreed upon between the importer and the exporter.

Transit shipment—A term designating a shipment destined for an interior point or a place best reached by reshipment from another point.

Trust receipt—Release of merchandise by a bank to a buyer in which the bank retains title to the merchandise. The buyer who obtains the goods for manufacturing or sales purposes is obligated to maintain the goods (or the proceeds from their sale) distinct from the remainder of his/her assets, and to hold them ready for repossession by the bank.

Validated export license—A required document issued by the U.S. government to authorize the export of specific commodities. This license is for a specific transaction or time period in which the exporting is to take place. *Compare* General export license.

Warehouse receipt—A receipt issued by a warehouse listing goods received for storage.

a. Negotiable: Transferable by endorsement and requiring surrender of a receipt to the warehouseman for delivery of the goods.
b. Non-negotiable: Indicates the non-transferability of goods; goods will be delivered only to the person named therein or to a third party only on written order, such as a delivery order.

Wharfage—A charge assessed by a pier or dock owner for handling incoming or outgoing cargo.

Without reserve—A term indicating that a shipper's agent or representative is empowered to make definitive decisions and adjustments abroad without approval of the group or individual represented. *Compare* Advisory capacity.

INDEX

A

accounting practices, foreign, 15
advertising, 38, 40
Agency for International
 Development (AID),
 160–161
Albania, 10

B

banks and banking, 41, 43–47,
 50, 51, 53–54, 60-64, 72,
 86–87, 107–109, 110
barter, 111, 123
brand names, 81
Bulgaria, 10
Business Review Letter, 119

C

cash-in-advance, 85, 86, 106
catalogs, 59
certificate of origin, 92
China, 13
City-State Agency Cooperative
 Program, 47
collecting, problems with, 105,
 113
COMECON, 3, 9, 10
Commercial Bank Guarantee
 Program, 45
Commodity Credit Corpora-
 tion, 51–52
Commonwealth of Indepen-
 dent States, 11
communications, 64–65

competition, 23, 78
computers, 38–39
consignment, 85, 86, 106, 111
contacts, making, 69–70
contacts for export, 165–218
copyright protection, 14, 65, 120
countertrade, 111–112, 117, 123–124
credit, 72
Cuba, 10
currency, 6, 9, 10, 11, 54, 59, 87–88, 111, 112
Customs, 90
Czechoslovakia, 3, 8, 9–10, 13

D

documentation, 88–89
documents, government control, 90–92
demographic information, 23
documentary drafts, 85, 86, 87, 106, 109–110

E

Eastern Bloc, collapse of, 7–13
Eastern Europe, 5, 7, 111. *See also individual countries.*
 Western aid to, 12
 Western investment in, 11–13
East Germany, 8–9, 13
Engineering Multiplier Program, 46
Estonia, 11
European Bank for Reconstruction and Development in Eastern Europe, 11
European Currency Unit (ecu), 6
European Economic Community (EC), 2, 3–7, 14, 120, 122
European Free Trade Association (EFTA), 2
Export Administration Regulations, 67
export business
 costs of starting, 42–43
 entering, 20–40
 financing, 43–54
 getting started in, 55–74
 industries, opportunities for, 30–35
 managing, 75–104
 mistakes in, 27–28
 potential, researching, 24–26
 service industries and, 37–40, 120
 servicing of products and, 114–116
 setting up, 41–54
 state assistance for, 125–132
 strategy, outlining, 26–27
 U.S. corporations and, 17–18, 19–20, 35, 38, 52
 U.S. government assistance for, 145–163
Export Credit Guarantee Program, 51
Export Credit Insurance Program, 43–44
Export-Import Bank (Eximbank), 12, 43–47
Export Revolving Line of Credit Program, 50

Export Trade Certificate of Review, 119

F

Federal Laboratory Consortium for Technology Transfer, 161
Foreign Agriculture Service (FAS), 157–159
Foreign Credit Insurance Association, 43, 44–45
foreign exchange, 87–88, 112–113. *See also* currency.
foreign trade zone, 154–155
franchising, 38, 117, 120–124
freight forwarders, 84–85

G

General Agreement on Tariffs and Trade (GATT), 39
General Electric Co., 17–18
Georgia, Republic of, 11
Germany. *See* East Germany; West Germany.
government, U.S., stimulating exports and, 145–163
Gross Domestic Product, 14

H

Hungary, 3, 8, 13

I

insurance
  cargo, 90
  credit risk, 72, 113
International Chamber of Commerce, 74, 113
International Trade Administration, 125, 151, 152–154
invoices, 79–80

J

Japan, 3, 5, 7, 8, 12, 15, 36
joint ventures, 117, 118

K

Korea, 15

L

Latvia, 11
legal services, 67, 119
letter of credit, 72, 85, 86–87, 106, 106–109
licenses, export, 67–69
licensing, 117, 119–120
Lithuania, 11

M

manufacturing facilities, overseas, 117, 118
market demand, 78
market research, 21, 23, 37, 126
metric sizing, 35
Mongolia, 10

N

National Marine Fisheries Service, 155

O

office, setting up, 63–67
open account, 85, 86, 106, 110–111
Organization of Economic Cooperation and Development (OECD), 2, 22
Overseas Private Investment Corp., 12, 47–49

P

packaging and shipping, 81–84
patents, 14, 39–40, 65–66, 120
payment, terms of, 85–88, 105–113
Poland, 7–8
price/earnings ratios, 15
pricing for export market, 70–72, 75–80

R

re-export, 117
regulations, 29, 36, 119
Romania, 10
royalties, 119
Russia, Republic of, 11

S

sale, terms of, 80
sales facilities, foreign, 117, 118
servicing of products, 114–116
Single Internal Market: 1992 Information Service, 4–5
Small Business Credit Program, 46
small business innovation research grants, 50–51
states, U.S., stimulating exports and, 126–132
    offices, list of, 127–132, 165–199
"stock pairing," 65

T

Taiwan, 15
taxes, 65, 154
trademarks, 14, 81, 120
trade shows, 55–59

U

U.N. Development Program, 37
U.S. Agency for International Development, 37
U.S. and Foreign Commercial Service (US&FCS), 126, 155–156
U.S. Customs Service, 162–163
U.S. Department of Agriculture, 157–159
U.S. Department of Commerce, 4, 18, 22, 27, 38, 40, 52, 56, 67, 68, 69, 112, 113–114, 119, 120, 125, 145, 151–156, 159
U.S. Department of Justice, 119
U.S. International Trade Commission, 161–161
U.S. Small Business Administration, 22, 46, 50, 51, 67, 145, 159–160

USSR, 10–11
U.S. Trade and Development
    Program, 49–50
U.S. Trade Representative, 3

V

Vietnam, 10

W

Western Europe, 13
    free-trade market and, 5
    investing in, 14
West Germany, 5, 7, 8, 9, 13, 14
World Bank, 37
Working Capital Co-Guarantee
    Program, 46
Working Capital Guarantee
    Program, 46

Y

Yugoslavia, 10

ABOUT THE AUTHOR

Roger Fritz writes and speaks from 40 years experience as an educator (Wisconsin and Purdue), a manager (Cummins Engine), corporate executive (John Deere), university president, and highly successful consultant to over 250 clients, including AT&T, Brunswick, IBM, Caterpillar, Dial, Motorola, Pizza Hut, Sara Lee, and scores of other corporations and organizations large and small. He has a Ph.D. from the University of Wisconsin and founded Organization Development Consultants in 1972. Dr. Fritz is the author of 26 books including *Performance Based Management, Productivity and Results, Rate Your Executive Potential, You're In Charge, Think Like A Manager, The Entrepreneurial Family,* and *How to Export: Everything You Need to Know to Get Started.* He has produced 25 audio albums and 2 video training series, and his skills are being utilized by 4 companies as a member of their board of directors.

In addition to his consulting work, Dr. Fritz conducts seminars and workshops.

Additional Titles of Related Interest Available from Probus Publishing

How to Sell Your Business for the Best Price (With the Least Worry!), Vaughn Cox

Entrepreneur's Guide to Capital, Revised Edition, Jennifer Lindsey

Forecasting Your Company's Sales and Profits (Quickly, Easily and Realistically!), Kenneth E. Marino

Cashflow, Credit and Collection: Over 100 Proven Techniques for Protecting and Strengthening Your Balance Sheet, Basil P. Mavrovitis

Funding Research & Development: How to Team Up with the Federal Government to Finance Your R & D, Patrick D. O'Hara

Initial Public Offerings: All You Need to Know About Taking A Company Public, David P. Sutton and M. William Benedetto

Mastering the Business Cycle: How to Keep Your Company on Track in Times of Economic Change, Albert N. Link

Negotiating a Bank Loan (You Can Live With!), Arthur G. Pulis III

Crafting the Perfect Name: The Art and Science of Naming a Company or Product, George Burroughs Blake and Nancy Blake-Bohné.

Telemarketing That Works: How to Create a Winning Program for Your Company, Raymond C. Harlan and Walter M. Woolfson, Jr.

Building a Winning Sales Team: How to Recruit, Train and Motivate the Best, Gini Graham Scott